Dan Erwin

$\frac{365}{9\sqrt{3}}$

D0765597

THE NEED TO PREACH

By the same author:

Published by Hodder and Stoughton, Harpers and the Ryerson Press:

BARRIERS TO CHRISTIAN BELIEF
THE ETERNAL LEGACY
THE CRUCIAL ENCOUNTER

Published by Hodder and Stoughton and Word Inc.:

GOD IN MAN'S EXPERIENCE
ILLUSIONS OF OUR CULTURE

Published by the Lutterworth Press, the Abingdon Press and the Ryerson Press:

GOD AND HIS PEOPLE
THE ROMAN LETTER TODAY
BENEATH THE CROSS OF JESUS
WHAT IS A CHRISTIAN?
GOD'S TIME AND OURS
THIS IS LIVING

Published by the Independent Press and the Abingdon Press:

PATHWAYS TO HAPPINESS

Published by the Epworth Press:

A PILGRIMAGE TO THE HOLY LAND

THE NEED TO PREACH

by

LEONARD GRIFFITH

HODDER AND STOUGHTON

LONDON   TORONTO   SYDNEY   AUCKLAND

For

George and Lucy Finch

Contents

Introduction

A daily newspaper,[1] which boasts the largest circulation in Canada, devoted a full-page symposium to the question, "What is the future of the sermon in today's changing church?" The object of the exercise was evidently to show that sermons of the traditional style are irrelevant in the modern Church and ought to be abandoned. The writers included a professor of New Testament, a Roman Catholic priest, two conservative Evangelicals and an internationally known evangelist who gave up preaching and dropped out of the Church more than ten years ago. There was also an article by a layman who believes that sermons by ordained ministers should give way to free-for-all dialogues and who frequently preaches sermons to prove it.

Mr. George Finch, a Methodist layman in North Carolina, holds a diametrically opposite viewpoint, though he does not ventilate it in the newspapers. He believes that preaching should be encouraged, not disparaged. He likes listening to sermons, not because it means that he can sit still while the preacher does all the work, but because sermons communicate to him a Word of God that instructs, inspires and enables him to practise the Christian life in his home and in the demanding world of business where he has achieved more than ordinary success.

When Methodist Bishop Earl Hunt Jr. expressed concern about the growing indifference of theological colleges and of ministers themselves to preaching he found a ready response from George

9

Finch. Together they established the Institute for Homiletical Studies which includes among other subjects an annual series of lectures on preaching to the ministers of the Western North Carolina Conference. Few people know that Mr. Finch and his wife bear the financial burden of these lectures. It is a case of putting money where the ear is – surely a Christian posture, if the ear is listening to God's Word.

On the invitation of Bishop Hunt I presented the Finch Lectures in January, 1970, and the text of them is contained in the following pages. It was a thrilling experience to speak four times to the audience of five hundred ministers and answer their questions which indicated that they still see more relevance in preaching than in the articles of journalists who seem determined to write its obituary.

Actually these lectures were born several years ago and delivered in infant form to the summer Institute of Theology at Princeton Theological Seminary. Revised for presentation in North Carolina, they were later given as the Chancellor's Lectures at Queen's University in Kingston, Canada. For publication the manuscript has been expanded to include four sermons preached in Deer Park Church, Toronto, which follow and grow directly out of Chapter Three, "Great Themes for Great Times".

As the general title suggests, there is still a need to preach. That need exists in the preacher himself who, if he obeys the Word of God, has no choice but to proclaim it faithfully. The need exists in Christian laymen who, if they want to hear the Word of God, must be willing to listen as well as talk. The need exists in the Church which, if it seriously hopes to share in the continuing ministry of Christ, must accept his direct, divine mandate to preach. The need exists in the world outside the Church which, as Paul said, will never hear the Gospel "without a preacher". The need to preach is inherent in the Gospel itself which is no Gospel unless the Word of God, incarnate in Christ and contained in Holy Scripture, is related, proclaimed and interpreted from the pulpit.

In a day when so many people inside and outside the Church seem anxious to proclaim the death of preaching I give thanks

Introduction

for encouragers of the pulpit like George and Lucy Finch. I thank all who have listened to these lectures or encouraged their publication, especially Mr. Edward England, Religious Editor of Hodder and Stoughton. I thank my secretary, Mrs. Isabelle Macklin, who typed the manuscript, and Mr. Charles Reid who kindly read and corrected the proofs.

The preparation of this book coincides with the twenty-fifth anniversary of my ordination as a Christian minister. In the course of that very exciting and challenging ministry I have been privileged to be the pastor of five churches and have preached to congregations in Canada, Britain, the United States and Australia. I have faced ten thousand people in a convention auditorium and three people in a country conventicle. I know the joys and the heartaches of a preacher, the exhilaration of a huge audience and the despondency of empty pews. I am fully aware of the rapid changes taking place in the Church and in secular society and I have run into all the obstacles that can kill the enthusiasm for preaching. Nevertheless I continue to preach because I need to preach, and I offer this book with the prayer that it will re-awaken the same need in many hearts.

LEONARD GRIFFITH

Toronto, 1970.

1   *Toronto Daily Star*, March 21, 1970.

11

CHAPTER ONE

The Un-making of a Preacher

PREACHING IN DECLINE

It is my task in these lectures to speak about the place of the preaching ministry in the Church. The first thing to be said is that the preaching ministry cannot and must not be separated from the total Church picture. That picture is not as bright as it was a generation ago. Whereas people used to ask how the Christian Faith helped them with the problems of life, now they are asking if the Christian Faith is true. Whereas the choice used to be between churches of different denominations, or even of the same denomination, now the choice is between Church and no-Church. The preaching ministry fits into that total picture of scepticism and decline. Instead of asking, "How shall we preach?" or "What shall we preach?", laymen, professors, seminarians and ministers are now asking, "Why should we preach?" and "Should we preach at all?"

In many quarters the answer to that question is a resounding "No". If we follow the advice of some modern gurus and prophets we shall not include sermons in our services of worship. Instead, we might distribute little white substances, not sacramental bread but harmless psychedelic drugs that will put us all into a trance and turn us on emotionally to a mystical experience of

12

God. Or we may engage in some form of mass hypnosis. There is an Episcopal priest in the United States who hypnotises his congregation every year on Good Friday. Holding a crucifix before them he intones, "You find yourself growing very sleepy. . . . your eyes are closing . . . . you are going backward in time, back, back, to the day of our Lord's death . . ." Well, some of you may find yourselves growing sleepy before I have finished lecturing, but the cause will be boredom, not hypnosis. And *that*, according to the experts in communication, is why we should stop preaching altogether. Sermons bore people. They stay away from Church because they are tired of listening to the spoken Word.

Within the Churches today many people of considerable influence sincerely believe that the age of preaching is dead. The argument is not simply that the Church no longer produces great preachers or that preaching has gone into a temporary eclipse from which it will emerge but that preaching in the classical tradition is no longer an effective or acceptable means of communicating the Gospel. Apparently we have to devise new methods of preachment – dialogues, group discussion, dramatic presentation, colourful liturgy, induced "happenings", etc., and all are being tried with varying degrees of success and failure.

This means that whoever presumes to lecture about preaching has to be more basic in his approach than the golf professional who takes it for granted that we enjoy the game and want to improve our score. That might be something of a relief. Many books and lectures on preaching simply irritate me. They do begin with the assumption of a golf professional – that I was incorrectly taught in the first place, that my techniques have been all wrong and my game abysmally poor (which may be true, so far as golf is concerned) and that I had better unlearn my mistakes and start again from scratch. The author or the lecturer is going to take me in hand, correct my grip on the subject, straighten the drive of my eloquence, change the swing of my ideas and show me how to keep my head down on the manuscript. He makes it quite clear that there are really only two ways to preach – his way and the wrong way. Today's preaching pro has a more basic assignment. He has to start further back and convince me, so that I can convince you, that it is worthwhile to continue playing the game of preaching at all.

"What will this babbler say?"

To that task I now address myself and in true homiletical style I begin by announcing a text of Scripture. These lectures and sermons attempt to expound the text and the incident that surrounds it. In the Acts of the Apostles it is reported that when Paul stood on Mars Hill in Athens and spoke to the philosophers, they asked this question about him: "What will this babbler say?" (Acts 17:18) It is a very real question in a company of preachers. Perhaps you are asking it about me now. You can be certain that people have asked it about you, not so patronisingly, perhaps, or so bluntly; but always in every congregation there are those who survey you critically as you stand up to preach the Word of God and who ask, in the back of their minds at least, "What will this babbler say?"

Let us put the question in its original setting. Flushed with success after completing the major part of his second missionary journey, the Apostle Paul came to Athens. In Asia Minor he had run into some frustrating obstacles, but there came to him in a dream the vision of a man who said, "Come over to Macedonia and help us" (Acts 16:9); and Paul saw before him an open door to the strategic centres of world civilisation. After crossing the Aegean Sea he landed at Philippi; and though his visit ended in expulsion from that city, he made some loyal converts and sowed the seeds of a strong Christian community. Similarly at Thessalonica and Berea he and his companions encountered violent opposition, but there again they left the Christian Faith solidly rooted. No intellectual pygmy himself, Paul must have tingled with excitement as he approached Athens, the intellectual capital of the ancient world, the city of Socrates and Plato. Here surely the Gospel would be heard with dignity and understanding. The Athenians were not vulgar people; they were not peasants. Eagerly Paul gravitated to the little groups of philosophers gathered in the market-place as curious people gather at the orators' corner in London's Hyde Park on a Sunday afternoon. Any lecturer could attract an audience in Athens. Some people derive pleasure from gambling, others from watching games, but the Athenians enjoyed an argumentative discourse. "What will *this* babbler say?" they asked themselves as Paul made ready to address them; and in a deference to his intellectual stature they brought him to the famous Areopagus, known as Mars Hill, and settled back critically to listen.

The Preacher

There are four things to notice about the Mars Hill incident: (1) the preacher, (2) the congregation, (3) the sermon, (4) the verdict. In this lecture we shall look at *the preacher*, God's spokesman announcing the Good News of Salvation. Paul was primarily a preacher. To whatever city he came in the Mediterranean world he went on the Sabbath Day to the synagogue and to an assembled crowd of Jews and Gentiles he proclaimed the everlasting Gospel. He was a great preacher. He possessed other gifts which any servant of God might well envy, gifts of scholarship, administration, healing, evangelism and pastoral care, but all of these he subordinated to the ministry of the spoken Word. Paul preached because he believed in preaching as the most effectual means of confronting men with Jesus Christ. He saw preaching as the essential witness without which all other forms of Christian witness and service are futile. To the Romans he wrote: "How are men to call upon him in whom they have not believed? And how are they to believe in him of whom they have never heard? And how are they to hear without a preacher?" (Rom. 10:14) Sometimes preaching seems foolish, and no one knew it better than Paul, yet he could still say, "It pleased God through the foolishness of preaching to save those who believe." (1 Cor 1:21)

So we begin where a consideration of the Church's preaching ministry must always begin – with the preacher himself, the "speaking man", as Carlyle called him. He is the man who stands before his fellow-men and presumes to speak to them on behalf of God. Karl Barth described him: "On Sunday morning when the bells ring to call the congregation and minister to church, there is in the air an *expectancy* that something great, crucial and even momentous is to happen ... And here above all is a *man*, upon whom the expectation of the apparently imminent event seems to rest in a special way . . . He will enter the pulpit and – here is daring! – *preach*."[1] We wonder how any flesh and blood man, possessed of the normal human frailties, could possibly display such daring. By what colossal conceit does he presume to be qualified to speak to men on behalf of God? What factors go into the making of an authentic preacher?

Suppose we turn the question around and approach it negatively. From many quarters we hear the complaint that preaching has become a lost art, that the Church today is not producing the masters of the pulpit who enthralled congregations of sermon-tasters a generation ago. That might be a good thing if it did away with "sermon-tasters", for they always remind me of tea-tasters who swill the liquid around in their mouths and then spit it out. For my part I should prefer to think that occasionally someone swallows one of my sermons, even though it may give him indigestion. Still, we cannot escape the charge that the pulpit has failed to reproduce itself and that we who speak for God today are not worthy successors of the preaching giants of the past. Charles Clayton Morrison, for many years editor of the *Christian Century*, disturbed our consciences when he wrote in his retirement:

"For a number of years I have been a modern Diogenes going about with my homiletical lantern in search of a preacher. When I found one, it was a rather exciting experience, because I found so few. The pulpit, which is the throne of Protestantism, seemed to have become the footstool of a new ruler – the Cult of Consultation. The sermon had lost its character as an Event, either for the preacher or the congregation. It had become hardly more than a space-filling homily in a highly liturgical or folksy impromptu exercise preparatory to the coffee break."

Did Dr. Morrison speak the truth? Can it be said that young men and women, ordained into the ministry today, lack the essential qualifications of preachers? If so, where does the fault lie? What are the factors that go into the un-making of a preacher?

16

The Un-making of a Preacher

One factor must surely be a failure on the part of the theological colleges to create competent preachers or even to create an enthusiasm for preaching. Here is a drama in two acts. Act One takes place in a classroom at a prominent Canadian college. The time is January, 1955. I have been invited to speak to the senior class about preaching; and though I am comparatively young and inexperienced, the students listen eagerly and fire at me a barrage of intelligent questions. It is evident that they want me to share with them everything that I have learned about the art of pulpit communication. Act Two takes place in the same classroom twelve years later. During the interval I have gained considerable experience and reputation as a preacher on three continents and am the author of ten volumes of sermons, but the members of the senior class are unimpressed. They are not only not interested in what I have to say about preaching; they are bored, almost hostile. The generation gap is a mile wide. They stare at me in stony silence. They regard me as a relic of the past, an extinct volcano; and their only question, which they ask in a variety of ways, is, "Why should we try to preach at all?"

Obviously the un-making of preachers begins in the colleges which either deliberately downgrade preaching or which are so exclusively academic or so socially or liturgically orientated in their emphasis that they relegate preaching to a place of secondary importance in the curriculum. That might not be true of the major seminaries in the United States which have large, well-staffed departments of homiletics. Students in many smaller colleges, however, if they receive any instruction in preaching at all, receive it from part-time tutors who, though expert in other fields, would rate last in the list of candidates for any vacant pulpit. The students at one college in Britain did some calculating and came up with the interesting fact that their four professors could boast a combined total of thirteen years of practical experience in the pastoral ministry. The assumption is that an ordinand, if he has been well tutored in the subject-matter of Christianity, will pick up the techniques of communicating it as he goes along. That assumption would have disastrous effects if it were adopted by a medical school which instructed doctors in the

17

theory of surgery and left it to them to pick up the surgical techniques as they went along.

Moreover, I can think of no form of instruction less calculated to produce effective preachers than the mutual-criticism sessions that comprise some courses in homiletics. If you want an amusing burlesque on this practice, try to imagine the disciples gathered in the upper room after the Day of Pentecost, all with notebooks in their hands and ready to tear Peter's sermon to shreds. John speaks up, "I don't wish to be unkind, Peter, but you spoke for too long. There are no souls saved after the first twenty minutes." Matthew chimes in, "You spoke too rhetorically, too theologically, with not enough contemporary illustrations." James adds his two-cents-worth, "I couldn't always follow the logic of your argument. It seems to me that the material might have been better arranged." Thomas sums it all up by saying, "I liked the sermon but I think you might have chosen a better text." Poor Peter! He thought he had done rather well in view of the three thousand decisions for Christ – a record which even Billy Graham has not equalled – but obviously, in terms of the homiletic art, his sermon had been a bad show, and he would have to do better next time.

We have only to study the curricula of the most progressive seminaries in order to discover the requisites for training effective preachers. First and most important, a course on the theory of preaching which includes lectures and tutorials that comprise every aspect of sermonising – its derivation, construction, language, illustration and delivery. Such a course should demand written assignments, always written, requiring the students to submit introductions, text-divisions, illustrations, conclusions and complete sermon manuscripts which shall be discussed with a tutor as meticulously as any assignment in New Testament or historical theology. Then should come courses of study on the great preachers and the great sermons which shall be read and dissected and analysed to expose the ingredients of their greatness – their loyalty to biblical ideas, their doctrinal soundness, the logicality of their thought, the concreteness of their language, their use of metaphor and illustration, their relevance to contemporary human need. Only then should students be encouraged to preach, and for pity's sake not before a critical audience of fellow-students pretending to be a congregation. The ideal congregation prays for a preacher; it does not punch holes in his discourse. Far better that a man address rows of empty pews – which he might do eventually anyway – or that the criticism be left entirely to the teacher.

Not for a moment do I propose that the colleges should in any way subordinate their academic integrity to a mere emphasis on techniques. Even in other fields we deplore the fact that some universities tend to graduate more technicians than educated men. But preaching is not a technique; it is a witness, the principal historic witness to God's great drama of redemption in Jesus Christ. In our Reformed and Free Church tradition the sermon is an event, *the* event in the weekly life of a fellowship of Christian people. No college or seminary can presume to have prepared a student for ordination unless, having educated him in academic and related disciplines, it has taught and equipped him to perform effectively the central function of the Church's ministry.

THE MAN HIMSELF

If preaching in the modern Church is on the decline, some of the blame must rest on preachers themselves. The truth is that many ministers could preach more effectively than they do if they were willing to pay the price. They have all the "charismatic" gifts – keen minds, eloquence, imagination, sensitivity – else they would not have graduated from seminary, but very often these gifts lie undeveloped like a well of oil which has never been tapped. It costs something to be a preacher. That is the whole burden of Paul's two letters to Timothy, which the servant of God should read unceasingly and even memorise, because Paul addressed them primarily to preachers, especially that verse which the King James version translates, "Neglect not the gift that is in thee, which was given thee by prophecy, with the laying on of the hands of the presbytery" (1 Tim. 4:14).

Peculiar perils attend the ordained ministry, and someone has reduced them to three – the temptation to shine, the temptation to whine, and the temptation to recline. That last-named peril, more bluntly described as the avoidance of hard work, can be the un-making of any preacher, whatever his God-endowed gifts. The problem is aggravated because external discipline is absent. Most men are subject to the oversight of managers and foremen and bosses and must therefore keep regular hours of work or lose their jobs. Even the self-employed man, the salesman, the farmer, the insurance agent or the author, is subject to economic discipline; if he doesn't work neither will he eat. At least, it used to be that way until governments began talking about a guaranteed annual wage. The ministry, however, is unique in this respect – that it is the one profession which a lazy, incompetent or unprincipled man can exploit for his own advantage and through which he can bluff his way for a lifetime. Let him compile a minimum of basic sermons to which he adds from time to time and, if he changes his pastorate often enough, he can enjoy a forty-year ministry without ever doing a hard day's work in his life. Only to God must he give account of his stewardship and, if he can square that with his conscience, he can get away with anything. Moreover, in these days people in the pews show a tolerance or an apathy that their grandfathers would never have shown. If their minister neglects one department of his work, they will give him the benefit of the doubt, assuming that other duties have prior claim on his time and energy. They might wish for a more sustaining diet from the pulpit on Sunday mornings but they are too indifferent or too loyal to say so. Speaking to the next-door neighbours, who belong to a rival congregation, they quickly spring to the defence of their spiritual leader by saying, "He is a good mixer. He really knows how to get along with young people. Preaching is not his strong point. He doesn't pretend to be a preacher" – which, of course, is exactly what he pretends to be.

One illusion that needs to be punctured, if the Church hopes to see a revival of the preaching ministry, is the mistaken idea that preachers are born, not made. You hear it said of a successful pulpiteer, "He is a born preacher. He speaks so effortlessly. The words just flow from his lips. He doesn't even have to work at it." The preacher replies with a smile, "That's what you think!" To be sure, some men do have a native eloquence, called colloquially "the gift of the gab". They can say and sometimes do say nothing exquisitely but they can't keep on saying nothing, because even the most doting congregation cannot be mesmerised indefinitely. In any pastorate, that lasts longer than a year or two, there comes a time when the man in the pulpit must have something worthwhile to say, or his people will cease to tolerate him. The truth is that no man pays a higher price for success than does the effective preacher who appears casual and relaxed and gives the impression that he is doing it without any effort. The chances are that beneath his relaxed exterior he is perspiring profusely, and it is certain that behind his casual presentation lies the discipline of sheer hard work.

Paul himself specified two conditions of effective preaching. In his Second letter to Timothy he wrote, "Study to shew thyself approved unto God, a workman that needeth not to be ashamed, rightly dividing the word of truth" (II. Tim 2:15). John Henry Jowett lived by that verse. At Carrs Lane Church in Birmingham he always reached his study by six a.m. so that he could hear the sound of men's boots on their way to work and remind himself that he also was a workman who needed not to be ashamed. The word to notice is "study". There are some professions where a man can pick up enough information in college or technical school to qualify him for a lifetime of work but they are becoming fewer, and the ministry has never been one of them. Seminary does no more than introduce us to the fields of religious knowledge, launching us on a discipline of study which must be continued until the day we retire. Every preacher knows from experience that as long as he studies he has something to say; the well is primed. Stop studying, and the well runs dry. He knows that he must give priority to his study of the Bible, not simply to find appealing texts on which to hang his own ideas but in order that he may discover and interpret Bible ideas, the Word of God as it speaks to the needs of his people and his generation. He will do his best to understand the contemporary theologians, not to appear erudite by dragging their names into his sermons but in order to tell his people what the Church is saying today, not what it said four hundred years ago. He will study the literature, the art, the journalism which comprise our culture, not to make a parade of sophistication but in order that he may know the situation in which men live and address God's Word to that situation.

The second condition of effective preaching, which Paul specifies in the phrase, "rightly dividing the word of truth", is meticulous preparation. It is said of some of the great preachers that they spent one hour preparing for every minute they spoke in the pulpit. That is not unreasonable when you remember that a prolific novelist like Arthur Haley (author of *Hotel* and *Airport*), after he has completed his research, writes in a full day the equivalent of only three type-written pages, double spaced. The prolific preacher pays a similar price. He may seem to be speaking "off the cuff", but that is only one of the tricks of his trade. When he steps into the pulpit he has his material organised down to the last detail; he knows exactly what he is going to say and even, perhaps, how he is going to say it. A case in point is G. A. Studdert-Kennedy, the famous chaplain of the First World War who held congregations of soldiers spellbound by his salty discourses. William Purcell writes of him:

"To most who heard him his speaking appeared to be brilliantly extempore. In fact, it was nothing of the sort. Meticulous preparation backed by a powerful memory was the essence of it. He once said he 'dared leave nothing to chance'... The price paid in labour was enormous, and it was scarcely surprising that those – and they were numerous – who tried to emulate his style so often failed not only because they lacked his unique fire, but also because they fell short of the rigorous preparation which was the price of its effectiveness."[2]

Much ought to be said about the devotional life and pastoral care as sources of effective preaching, but these and all other factors add up to the same thing – discipline and hard work. Let the preacher beware of those well-meaning friends who warn him against working too hard; they may be his worst advisers and may unconsciously want to drag him down to their own level of mediocrity. The truth is that few people in any vocation work too hard; few achieve their true work potential. Employing our time and energy wisely, we are capable of crowding far more into the average day than we imagine. Someone described Albert Schweitzer – who combined several careers and astonished people by his prodigious output of work – as a man who learned to use himself fully. We can describe many a poor preacher as a man who has not learned to use himself fully.

One Minister's Method

Let's see what bored the seminary students in Act Two of the little drama which I described a few moments ago. Their Homiletics Professor had asked me to tell them something about my own method of preparing sermons. I began by telling them that for many years I have planned my pulpit ministry far in advance and have tried to pattern it on the Bible, the Liturgical Calendar and the Doctrine of the Trinity. From September to Advent the theme is God the Father and is usually based on a specific area of the Old Testament. From Christmas to Easter the sermons derive from the Gospels and attempt to set forth God the Son. From Pentecost to the summer I preach from the Acts or the Epistles about God the Holy Spirit. Having decided well ahead of time what these areas shall be, I set up a general file for each of them. There are files also for the Festivals of the Christian Year, for other Special Sundays, for topical series and for miscellaneous sermons.

In the early summer, when parish life mercifully slows down, I begin the background work on all this material, studying the Scripture texts with the aid of commentaries until they yield sermon seed-thoughts that fairly cry out to be cultivated. Usually the supply exceeds the demand. Like a fruit farmer who prunes a peach tree, I have to discard many ideas so that a few may have room to grow. By midsummer the general files are bulging. I then make a master chart which shows all the preaching dates from September to the following June. Having regard to the Festival Sundays, I begin setting some titles over against the dates – a juggling process like arranging and rearranging coloured slides in an illustrated lecture. When the plan is complete – as a guide and not as a tyrant – I then set up a separate file for each sermon, and it becomes a collector of pertinent materials until that sermon is ready to be written. In fact, that is one secret of effective illustration in preaching. It is astonishing how quick you are to make a record of newspaper articles, book references, current events and casual conversations when they seem to fit perfectly into sermons which you intend to preach at some future date.

Here is how the plan operates from week to week. On Friday morning, ten days in advance of the sermon deadline, I bring out the file and re-examine the idea and materials. That can be a disenchanting exercise, because an idea that sparkled like a diamond a few months ago may now have lost its lustre and seem like frosted glass. That calls for rearrangement or substitution. I ask two questions about a potential sermon idea – Is it a Word of God that speaks to a real situation? Can it be developed into a sermon that will preach? To answer both questions I have to get busy with pencil and paper and send up a number of trial balloons in the form of tentative outlines. If the idea does meet both conditions, I commit myself to its preparation, choose suitable hymns and plan the other details of the worship service.

Unless the pressure of parish duties dictates otherwise, I try to follow nine steps in the preparation of a sermon: (1) Steep my mind in the Scripture, the commentaries, the book references, the illustrative material; then lay them aside and think about them until their thoughts blend with mine. (2) Make a bare sermon outline with no direct reference to the background materials, so that it shall be my outline and not someone else's. (3) Prepare a detailed outline of every paragraph and sentence, filling in quotations and illustrative materials as they serve and light up the main theme. This is the most important step, and I try to take it early in the week so as to allow time for reflection and revision. (4) Write the manuscript in pencil, using an eraser frequently, and, if time allows, at one sitting. (5) Re-write the manuscript on a typewriter, polishing the phrases and trying to make the language live. (6) Memorise the sermon, underlining key words with a red pencil. (7) Transfer the red pencil notes to a small notebook for use in the pulpit. (8) Spend a period of brooding, usually on Sunday morning, to recapture the original inspiration of the sermon, to see it in its wholeness, to plan its strategy of presentation and to grasp its purpose. (9) Offer the sermon to God and pray that he will accept it and make it his Word.

The Un-making of a Preacher

THE CHURCH
Secularisation

There are certain factors within the Church itself that contribute to the unmaking of preachers. One of them is a creeping secularisation. Instead of standing over against the secular culture, the Church too easily becomes co-extensive with the secular culture and entirely dominated by its standard of values. To an alarming degree that has happened in North America over the past twenty years. The Church has become very worldly, especially in its passion for publishing comparative statistics. A denomination maintains its headquarters like a big business corporation, with innumerable departments staffed by permanent executives and computers, which bombards its retail outlets with an unceasing barrage of directives and schemes designed to increase sales. A local congregation may groan under the pressure of these comparative statistics or it may develop an unchristian pride in its own achievements. Inevitably the character of the ministry has changed within this situation, and that is why many of the younger ministers are rebelling against it and opting out. The man of God who was once a scholar, prophet and pastor, has now become a sort of club manager whose main function is to direct the religious programme and raise money and generally keep the enterprise moving successfully. In that situation the most qualified minister may be one whom I met in the western United States. On his office wall, alongside his theological diplomas, he displays the more useful diplomas in Law and Business Administration.

The dilemma facing the average parish minister is that he has neither the time nor the energy to develop himself as a preacher. Even as he takes charge of his initial pastorate the hierarchy of priorities becomes apparent: first, administration; next, pastoral care; then, denominational duties; after that, sermonising; finally if there is any time left, reading and study. Every minister knows the pattern. On Monday morning he begins the week resolved to spend some time with C. H. Dodd and lay a solid exegetical foundation for next Sunday's sermon. He has scarcely settled himself at the desk when the telephone rings, calling him out on a case of bereavement. By Tuesday evening the committee meetings are in full swing, so he forgets Dodd and, after the Saturday wedding, puts the finishing touches to the little homily which he will deliver next morning in place of a sermon. In December, 1955, *Life* magazine, in its presentation of the world's great religions, devoted an entire issue to Christianity. Portraying a typical Protestant minister engaged in his weekly duties, it showed him writing his sermon under the light of a lamp at midnight. I hope his congregation saw that picture and felt ashamed. What other man in any profession is allowed only the fag end of his time and energy for his major task?

A minister may have a loyal, attentive and spiritually minded congregation, yet one which in its total attitude makes it impossible for him to conduct a faithful pulpit ministry. The odd thing is that his people may have called him mainly for his prowess in the pulpit. Cautiously they sent a committee to hear him preach. The cautious committee, according to a witty observer, looked as inconspicuous as a herd of elephants hiding behind a cabbage leaf. Having got their hooks into him as a prospective candidate, they invited him to preach in their own church; and on the basis of that one sermon, disregarding his past record as a leader of men and shepherd of souls, they called him to be their minister. But here is the strange paradox: once having got him inside, because he appeals to them as a preacher, they then proceed to destroy him as a preacher. They lay on his conscience so many burdens, which are unrelated to the pulpit, that it becomes impossible for him to read and study and grow intellectually. He scarcely has time to say his prayers. One day, to the astonishment of all, he suffers a nervous breakdown or announces his intention to seek a change in pastoral relationship – and they never guess the reason why.

The Strange World of the Bible

Preaching in the modern Church is discouraged also by the fact that a minister and his congregation usually inhabit different worlds of thought. Not many people attended a preaching mission that I once conducted in Belfast, so I realised that, if I wanted to meet the Irish in bulk, I had better go where they lived and worked. The logical place was the shipyard. For me it was like stepping into another world, a strange and exciting world. I understood the Irish brogue easily enough, but the technical terms which I heard in the slips, the cutting sheds, the engine works and the scientific laboratories sounded like phrases from a foreign language. My guide apologised for it, but I told him not to be sorry and remarked that some of the men working in the shipyard would probably find my world as strange as I found theirs.

Not all preachers are aware of it, and a few will not face up to it, but the truth is that they do live in a world of thought which is just as strange and foreign to their own congregations as the shipyard was to me. On Sunday morning the preacher emerges from his study steeped in the Bible, the commentaries, the devotional classics and the thoughts of the theologians. He has been living in that world all week. Its ideas are native to his mind. His people emerge from a world that in work is materialistic and in leisure mostly trivial. Perhaps they are better educated than congregations of former years, but only in the narrow sense of possessing enough specialised knowledge to equip them for the job of earning a living. In religion they are almost illiterate. They do not think nor are they prepared to think spiritually. The great words of the faith – God, holiness, sin, redemption, grace – fall on their ears like phrases from a foreign tongue which someone has called "Christianese". Such words cannot have for them the acquired meaning which they have for those who ponder them daily. Mentally there is a wide gulf fixed between preacher and congregation, and the existence of that gulf has robbed present-day preaching of much of its power.

To be more specific, the only great preaching is expository preaching, the faithful interpretation of God's Word in the Bible as it speaks to the needs of the individual and society. The topical or so-called "Life Situation" preaching, which has unfortunately become fashionable in recent years, may attract crowds and popularise a preacher for a while but it does not build up the Church. In the last analysis it does not create stable Christians. Unhappily an uphill task confronts the minister who resolves to preach to his people from "the strange world of the Bible", simply because the Bible has become a strange world to them. Once the

Bible was a layman's book. Its phrases, ideas and thought-forms were familiar to all Church members, and the preacher could take for granted a foundation of Scriptural literacy on which to build. Now the Bible, the least-read best-seller, has become a closed book again, the private preserve of the clergy; and congregations not only fail to appreciate expository preaching but sometimes resent it. Therefore the minister who wants to be an immediate success faces the temptation to compromise his theological integrity and give people the preaching pabulum that they apparently want. It all gives rise to a vicious circle – superficial ministers creating superficial congregations, and spiritually illiterate congregations ruining their preachers.

THE SOCIAL SITUATION

Yet, the Church, as such, must not be held entirely responsible for the un-making of preachers. As an institution in society the Church to some extent reflects the social situation; and factors that discourage the preaching ministry are present in the Church only because they are present on a much larger scale in the whole of society.

Communication

One such factor is the change in people's response caused by new methods of communication. People don't read the news any more; they listen to it on the radio while they are driving their cars or setting the dinner table. They don't read a novel; they wait for it to be made into a motion picture or else skim through a digest of it in a popular magazine. Television has so conditioned their minds to instantaneous images and pictorial presentations that they have not the patience to sit still and listen to a sustained linear discourse from a man cloistered in a crow's-nest pulpit. If they come to Church they want the worship of God to be short and snappy. They will listen attentively at the outset, but let the preacher go beyond what they judge to be a tolerable time-limit, and immediately they show signs of restlessness as though they have switched off and begun thinking about the Sunday dinner or their plans for the remainder of the day. Today the stop-watch tyrannises the pulpit, and that can be intimidating to the preacher. How can the true prophet proclaim faithfully the Word which God has given him when he sees squirming in the pews impatient people who judge the value of his message not by its quality but by its brevity? How can he continue to preach when he is not even sure if his people want him to preach?

Participation

Another factor that discourages preaching is participation. The demand for participation in the decision-making process is one of the most revolutionary factors of our time. It is toppling governments all over the world, shaking universities, destroying inherited privileges, fomenting labour strife, altering race relations and breaking up families. Roman Catholics can tell us what it means in terms of the revolt of clergy against bishops and bishops against the Pope. In Protestant churches it means that ordained ministers have been pulled down from the pedestal of authority and are being regarded less as leaders of laymen and more as servants who are paid to implement the decisions and lead the discussions of laymen. In fact, the ministry as such is being phased out in that many ministers themselves no longer regard their calling as special, sacred or even essential to the life of the Church. Obviously the pulpit has been stripped of much of its authority, and the only sermon that commands a hearing is one that takes the form of a dialogue between preacher and congregation. At least the preacher had better make it seem like a dialogue. No more dogmatic pronouncements, no more strong assertions, no more "Thus saith the Lord!" Now it has to be "in my opinion" and "it seems to me" and "I hope you will agree, but if you don't agree, your opinions are as good as mine". In that situation what is the point of preaching at all? People can be forgiven for refusing to respond to an authoritarian pulpit, but preaching does not have much future if they cease to respect the authority of God's Word in Scripture as it comes to them through the well-furnished and disciplined mind of their minister.

Leisure

Another factor in society that militates against the pulpit is increased leisure time. Most ministers, when they decided to enter the ministry, did so because they fully expected that their primary role in the Church would be to preach. Their lengthy and expensive training at university and seminary prepared them primarily to preach. At least it gave content to their sermons. It presupposed, however, that they would have somebody to preach to. It presupposed that the preacher would get a hearing. It presupposed that there would be people in church on Sundays. Until recently the people were in church. Now they have so much money to spend and so many things on which to spend it and so much leisure time in which to enjoy them that their lives have fallen into a new pattern from which the public worship of God is virtually excluded. In the part of the world where I live the change brought about by increased leisure time expresses itself in a phrase which you hear on people's lips as early as Thursday evening – "Have a nice weekend!" We never heard that phrase when we were young, because there were no weekends as we know them. You worked till Saturday noon; you might or might not own a car; you opened your summer home (if you had one) only in the summer; you went north in the winter only if you were young and south only if you were retired. You went to church on Sundays, because there wasn't much else to do on Sundays except go to church. Now we have the new phenomenon of people who retain their membership in a church, support that church, make its decisions and play an active part in its mid-week programme but who are rarely home on Sundays to join in the church's worship. We have church members who know their minister as a pastor and congregational leader but who rarely hear him preach; in fact, they want from their minister every kind of service except the service that he is trained and best qualified to give. Could anything be more calculated to un-make him as a preacher?

Indifference

More serious still is the sheer indifference of society as a whole to the Church's preaching ministry. At a top-drawer social function in London, England, I was introduced to a distinguished member of the British Parliament who, hearing that I was minister of the City Temple, remarked, "Ah yes! The City Temple! I was a pew-holder there in the days of R. J. Campbell." Then he murmured, "That's when people listened to sermons. It's a pity they don't listen to them now." He was right. People do not throng the City Temple or any other church today. They don't listen to sermons. Many of them don't even know that sermons are still being preached. They are indifferent to the Church's preaching ministry because they are indifferent to the Church itself. In large areas of the world, some of them the former strongholds of Christianity, the majority of people, even of those who believe in God, stand outside the orthodox community of faith altogether. They may be of the upper classes who retain their ancestral connection with the Church only for the sake of social respectability. They may be intellectuals or pseudo-intellectuals who have decided that the Church is irrelevant. They may be labourers, belonging to that lost province of Christianity which the Church never really captured. They may be of the new bourgeoisie, excited by their growing affluence but utterly materialistic in their thinking and so indifferent to the Church that they have even forgotten the name of the church they stay away from. If we cannot be cheerful about the Church's preaching ministry today, it is not because we are pessimists at heart, but only because we cannot separate it from the darkening shadows of the total Church picture.

CHAPTER NOTES
1 Karl Barth, *The Word of God and the Word of Man* (Harper, New York, 1957), pp. 104–106.
2 William Purcell, *Woodbine Willie* (Hodder and Stoughton, London, 1962), pp. 159–60.

CHAPTER TWO

The Pulpit in the Pew

THE LOST GLORY OF PREACHING

Dr. Thomas Jessop, Professor of Philosophy at the University of Hull and a distinguished Methodist layman, has written a number of helpful books on spiritual themes. In one of them there is a chapter entitled, "Listening to Sermons". He bemoans the fact that the glory has gone out of pulpit oratory. He believes that the present-day sermon is as good as the usual sermon of the nineteenth century, yet it plainly does not have the same effect. It is not an event in people's lives. They do not think or talk about it afterwards. Effective preaching demands two conditions: a good preacher, and a good congregation. There must be a bond of sympathy and understanding between the two, but the bond seems to have been broken, and Dr. Jessop blames the congregation for breaking it. He says:

"Our fault is in the lack of active participation. In the best of the old days, the sermon opened in an atmosphere of tense expectancy ... Our fathers did not come to church merely to sit and listen and receive. They threw themselves into the service ... The sermon was felt, not as a one-sided discourse but as an eager conversation in which all took part, the reciprocity loosening at the same time the preacher's tongue and the congregation's spiritual energies . . . The church contracted, the pews moved up to the pulpit and the pulpit slipped into every pew ... The glory that has gone out of preaching is the glory of communion. All the effort of preaching is left to the preacher, all the thinking, and all the yearning; the pew is not playing its part."[1]

In the first lecture we looked at some of the factors that go into the un-making of a preacher. One of them is the Church. A congregation that secularises its minister, forces him into the mould of an ecclesiastical business manager, compels him to say what simply rearranges its own prejudices and demands from him nothing but short, snappy homilies in a nervously clocked hour of religious entertainment may do more to destroy his integrity as a preacher than all the other factors combined.

Yet the converse may be equally true. Here and there one encounters a mature community of Christian people who honour the preaching of God's Word as the central event and motive-power in their life as a congregation. Not only do they respect the demands which the pulpit makes upon their minister, not only do they afford him sufficient time for study and sermon preparation; they positively encourage him to conserve his major energies for the pulpit ministry. Moreover, they *allow* him to preach – which means that they respond articulately to the Word of God rightly divided, voicing their appreciation when he compels them to come to grips with the deep issues of the Faith. Nothing so excites them as the lucid presentation of Christian doctrine and the fresh exposition of the Bible. They may even ask for "homework" assignments in order to study for themselves during the week the great passages of Scripture which their minister expounds on Sunday morning. In such an ideal situation even a man with comparatively few homiletic gifts grows and develops as a preacher.

Preaching is a Corporate Act

Some years ago an eminent Scottish preacher prefaced a sermon with the prayer: "O Lord, teach us to remember that for every sermon we *hear* we must render an account on the Day of Judgment." He prayed with right instinct. Ministers, of course, should render account to God for all the sermons they preach, and any honest preacher will confess that the awareness of that accountability does weigh heavily on his heart. Hearers of sermons

33

C

also should be held accountable, because preaching which effects a true divine-human encounter is a joint enterprise. It is an act not only of the man in the pulpit but of the whole Church. Henry Sloane Coffin defined preaching as "a corporate action in which preacher, congregation, and a long line of predecessors reaching back through the centuries to the original event and corroborating the interpretation of that event in the Scriptures, co-operate."

Jesus began his preaching ministry by enunciating that very truth in his familiar parable of the soils (Mark 4:1-20); and perhaps any minister, as he enters a new pastorate, could no better than expound this parable in one of his first sermons. It conveys the truth that there is a pulpit in the pew and that in the Church's preaching ministry hearing plays as important a role as speaking. The sower broadcasts the seed of God's Word but he knows from experience that it takes root only in the soil which has been prepared to receive it. How quickly we recognise those other soil types in our congregations: the closed, calloused, comfortable minds that simply resist divine truth; the shallow minds that respond with immediate enthusiasm but shrivel for want of deep experience; the cluttered minds, so overgrown with worldly cares that the Word of God has no room to grow. Yet we persevere in preaching because there is still the good soil, receptive in varying degrees, bringing forth fruit, thirty-fold, sixty-fold and a hundred-fold.

In the Acts of the Apostles there is a dramatic incident that shows preaching to be a joint enterprise between minister and congregation. Peter had been staying at Joppa where he saw an unforgettable and meaningful vision on the rooftop of the house of Simon the tanner. Soon afterwards he received visitors, a delegation from a Roman centurion in Caesarea named Cornelius who asked Peter if he would come to Caesarea and be his guest. As a devout Jew Peter had never before entered the house of a Gentile. In Cornelius' home he faced a congregation of Gentiles who received him cordially and sympathetically and said to him, "And now we are all met here before God, to hear all that the Lord has ordered you to say." (Acts 10:33) Peter preached to them and "was still speaking when the Holy Spirit came upon all who were listening to the message." The effect of that sermon was so revolutionary that it altered the whole course of early Christianity and ultimately changed the history of the world.

It was an ideal situation – the preacher himself, possessed by the Holy Spirit, speaking to a receptive congregation possessed by the same Spirit; and Spirit meeting with Spirit, the Word was proclaimed. I had been the minister of a church for several years before I learned that every Sunday morning a little group of devout women assembled in one of the deserted classrooms to invoke the presence and power of the Holy Spirit on that day's worship; though I really ought to have known it because sometimes I felt so strong in the pulpit that I could have said with Martin Luther, "I knew that I was being prayed for." How happy the preacher whose people, instead of sitting passively like spectators, uphold him with their prayers and take the attitude, "Now we are all met here before God to hear all that the Lord has ordered you to say."

Paul's Congregation

That hardly describes the congregation which Paul had the misfortune to face on Mars Hill in Athens. It was entirely unlike any that the apostle had ever addressed before. To begin with, the very surroundings were unfavourable to a proclamation of the Gospel, for the little mound of rock on which Paul preached was as dwarfed by the towering pagan Parthenon as an English Nonconformist Chapel is dwarfed by a nearby Anglican Cathedral, and his hearers were well aware of the contrast. Today we might call these people "eggheads", if they really deserve the name. Philosophers of the secondhand variety, they basked in the afterglow of Athens' intellectual glory. They lived on lectures. They fed on a diet of speculation, argument and discussion. They dealt in ideas as other people deal in produce and property and, when this little fiery Jew stood up to address them, they regarded him as if he were just another professional pedlar of ideas. "What will this babbler say? ... What new thing will he tell us to whet our intellectual appetites?" Outwardly, of course, the Athenians could claim to be very religious, as evidenced by the profusion of monuments and shrines that blocked the visitor's path wherever he walked through the streets of Athens, but it was a religion of cultural identification with no more relation to real life than a painting by Picasso has to a woman dying of cancer. Such was Paul's congregation on Mars Hill, and by and large it is still the most difficult and obstinate audience that a Christian preacher can face. Its resistance lies not in the roar of angry beasts but in the hard, unyielding quality of block marble.

How significant that, of all the cities which Paul visited, Athens should be the one where he failed to sow the seeds of a Christian Church! We search the New Testament in vain for a letter to the Athenians. From Athens, a city renowned for its learning, Paul moved on to Corinth, a city notorious for its vice; and the amazing thing is that in that tough and dissolute seaport Paul found such fertile ground for the Gospel that he remained there eighteen months, did some of his most fruitful work, established one of his strongest churches and subsequently addressed to the Corinthians his lengthiest letters. The Corinthians listened to Paul out of a sense of personal need. The Athenians listened with academic interest; in their very intellectual pride they were actually fighting him in everything he had to say.

Audience-Appeal

The fault may not have been altogether with Paul's hearers. It is just possible that the Apostle himself was partly to blame. There are times when a congregation can be forgiven for refusing to respond to a sermon. Perhaps the preacher says nothing to which they can respond, or says it so ambiguously that they don't know what he is talking about. Granted that preaching is an act of the whole Church and that the congregation has a role to play, it is up to the preacher to arrest the attention of his hearers and encourage them to play that role. His sermon must possess a quality which artists of the stage would call "audience-appeal".

Successful artists of the stage have a great deal to teach preachers, especially in their appreciation of the role played by an audience. In her autobiography, Marian Anderson, the great Negro contralto who succeeded phenomenally not only as a singer but as a person, acknowledges a profound debt to her audiences:

"Call it, if you like, radiation. You may go to a concert feeling below par. As you step out on the stage your audience's eagerness to hear and accept you before you have uttered a sound is a lift. You sense yourself being pulled up abruptly, and as you sing you find more and more strength coming to you from the audience. By the end of the evening the concert that you feared would not be much has turned out to be one of your best."[2]

That strikes an answering chord in the preacher's heart. He also can tell of occasions when he entered the pulpit feeling below par, and the eagerness of the congregation so lifted him that the sermon which he feared would not be much turned out to be one of his best. Miss Anderson goes on to say:

"I have never been able to analyse the qualities that the audience contributes to a performance. The most important, I think, are sympathy, open-mindedness, expectancy, faith, and a certain support to your efforts. I know that my career could not have been what it is without all these things which have come from many people. The knowledge of the feelings other people have expended on me has kept me going when times were hard. That knowledge has been a responsibility, a challenge, and an inspiration. It has been the path to development and growth. The faith and confidence of others in me have been like shining, guiding stars."[3]

But Marian Anderson never took her audiences for granted. She was too much of a professional for that. She knew that it rested with her, the singer, to make a contact with her audience and that this called for the exercise of her highest professional skills. She knew that she must always give her best performance, even though she felt unprepared and even though the audience appeared small and unresponsive. She must never "feel cocky or blasé before an appearance" but must step on the stage in fear and trembling. She must choose her programme carefully and master it perfectly, yet she must never lose spontaneity but "must leave something to be achieved at the performance, whatever that magical thing is". Above all, she must study the people in front of her and try to make out the expression on their faces and develop a knack of finding the people who are with her and sometimes pick out an individual or a group to whom to sing. Miss Anderson's book should be required reading for every course in homiletics.

Preaching, like singing, needs a quality of professionalism, especially in these days when radio and television have conditioned people to the best in all forms of art and communication. There might have been a time when a preacher, if he were sincere, could get away with a poor pulpit performance, but standards have changed, and people are critical. They are no more patient with the pulpit amateur than they are with dramatic amateurs presenting *The Merchant of Venice* on a makeshift stage. To establish rapport a sermon must have audience-appeal. We shall consider some of the factors that give it such appeal.

SUITED TO CONGREGATION

To have audience-appeal a sermon must be suited to a congregation. It must be tailored to a particular congregation. It must speak to *that* congregation. Ideally a community of Christian believers should represent a cross-section of society, embracing young and old, rich and poor, management and labour, educated and uneducated, but that is rarely possible in a society where other relationships are so stratified. As long as we have slums and country clubs, working-class areas and middle-class suburbs, inner cities and rural villages, we shall have churches that reflect the same secular grouping. Congregations, like people, have personalities, and it is a mistake to suppose that a preacher can serve all of them on the same diet of homiletic food. Congregations differ, and the sermon that rings the bell with one congregation may sound utterly dead to another.

We suspect that Paul's sermon on Mars Hill was not suited to his congregation. He was a great preacher, yet on this one occasion he seemed to have misjudged his congregation and blundered homiletically. Why did he depart in Athens from his usual straightforward approach? Did the Greek philosophers intimidate him, so that somehow he felt obliged to be tactful and highbrow and quote their poetry and meet them on their own scholarly ground? Halford Luccock recounts the stout legend that a young scientist, called upon to perform some experiments before Queen Victoria, thus explained the process: "The oxygen and hydrogen will now have the honour of combining before Your Majesty." They appreciated the honour and combined. In like manner, says Dr. Luccock, preachers have often said no less ingratiatingly of the Gospel, "The elements of revelation will now have the honour of combining to fit the ultimate majesty, the spirit of the time, the mood of the moment."[4] Was Paul too ingratiating on Mars Hill? He knew better than anyone that the obsequious approach does not start much of a fire burning in people's hearts. Wherever else he preached he came directly to the point. Instead of leading his listeners from their own presuppositions to the truths of the Gospel, he usually began with the truths of the Gospel – the life, death and resurrection of Christ – and on the basis of those truths challenged people to alter their presuppositions. For some reason he changed his technique in Athens, and his sermon fell flat. He didn't get the wave-length of his hearers; he failed to establish rapport with his congregation.

It is possible, of course, that Paul, regardless of what he said, was himself not suited to serve the sophisticated philosophers in Athens. That may seem odd in view of Paul's massive mind, but the fact that a man is something of a scholar does not necessarily mark him out as the ideal minister for a congregation of intellectuals. Of all British Prime Ministers William Ewart Gladstone possessed the greatest intellectual gifts. He would have preferred the academic life and he spent much of his spare time translating and writing essays on the Greek poets. Therefore it seemed altogether natural that in Parliament he should represent the university constituency of Oxford. Yet, strangely enough, Gladstone never achieved full stature as a statesman until he relinquished Oxford and contested a seat in Lancashire. Somehow those unsophisticated mill-workers of the north drew from him the very human qualities that made him great. Somehow he understood them, and they understood him. We saw that even Paul, for all his intellectual prowess, preached more successfully to the artisans of Corinth than to the philosophers in Athens.

It is an illusion to suppose that a preacher who ministers successfully to one segment of society can minister with equal success to others. You do have an occasional genius who in every circumstance can get inside people and speak to the human heart, a man who, like Paul, can *claim* to be "all things to all men". Most of us, however, find that we can reach certain types more effectively than we can reach others. God has equipped us for a ministry to farmers or business executives or factory workers or college students or retired people or city transients, and it is the path of wisdom to discover and, if possible, serve the kind of pastorate to which we are most suited. Not economic considerations, not the attraction of urbane people, not the proximity of educational facilities, not the interests of his own family should determine a minister's choice of a church but the simple consideration: "Is this where God wants me to be? Is this where I can most fruitfully serve him and where God can put my peculiar gifts to their fullest use, giving me a sense of accomplishment in my ministry?"

A Personal Experience

In 1960 I took the leap of faith and emigrated from North America to Britain. After eleven years in a large Canadian pastorate I felt confident that I had a substantial barrel of old sermons on which to draw but I quickly discovered how few of them were suited to the new situation. Just before making the move I had preached both in Canada and in the United States what seemed to be a well-worked-out series of five sermons on the Book of Job. Thinking that the theme of innocent suffering might appeal to a nation still smarting under wounds of war, I trotted out the series on Sunday evenings during my first month at the City Temple in London. I ought to have known better. When the play "J.B.", which is a modern adaptation of Job and which ran successfully for a year on Broadway, appeared in London's West End it lasted exactly three weeks and lost five thousand pounds. Of course my series went up like a lead balloon for the obvious reason that it lacked audience-appeal. It was more suited to a settled congregation than to a procession of itinerant worshippers. It assumed a knowledge of the Bible and a recognition of its authority which most of the people simply did not possess. The faithful few stuck by me to the bitter end, but the audiences shrank, and one curious spectator wrote nastily, "It is obvious that we are not going to get anything out of your ministry."

When I left the City Temple in 1966 and returned to take a grass-roots parish in Canada, an American Methodist minister, whom I have never met, wrote me a letter asking the bare-faced question which even my close friends were too tactful to ask – "Why did you do it?" I sent him a courteous reply to the effect that it was none of his business, but the truth is that I could not have answered his question at the time. In retrospect and with some detachment I realise that the City Temple is an unusual church. It has some two hundred active members who loyally and faithfully travel to worship Sunday after Sunday from all points of the compass in greater London. Essentially, however, its survival depends on filling at least half of the 1,400 seats twice each Sunday with audiences of visitors and occasional worshippers, many of whom have never heard the minister before and will never hear him again. It is like a permanent Billy Graham Crusade without Billy's machinery. In that situation a preacher needs peculiar gifts. He must have popular appeal. He must be able to seize on timely topics especially of a controversial nature. He must have a flair for publicity and he must know how to pack the whole Gospel into every sermon. Some preachers flourish in the City Temple situation and are ideally suited to it. I found it challenging, even exciting, but in the long run I am essentially a pastoral preacher. My sermons tend to be expository, doctrinal and liturgical. On any Sunday I am at home with people who heard me last Sunday and will hear me next Sunday and who set my sermon not only in the context of a total pulpit ministry but in the context of a total pastoral ministry. That is not to say that all of my sermons fell flat in the City Temple. A few rang a bell, but the majority were more suited to a settled congregation than to an audience of itinerant worshippers. I believe that every preacher ought to make that kind of self-assessment if he wants his preaching to be a joint enterprise with the congregation.

INTERESTING TO THE CONGREGATION

To have audience appeal a sermon must be interesting. Blessed-
ly we have outgrown the illusion that dullness in the pulpit is
a sign of erudition. There was a day when worshippers expected
their minister to be slightly over their heads and even boasted
that his pearls of vague theological jargon set him apart as "a
scholarly man". If he seemed too scholarly and too obtuse, they
excused him gently by saying, "Our minister is really very brilliant. He should be in a theological college" – which gives point
to the old saying that a man qualifies for a college chair by empty-
ing the pews of two churches. Still, it seems rather unfair that
the minister who bores his congregation should necessarily be in-
flicted on young men who are training for the ministry. Is it not
probable that he will bore them too and that some of them may
even be infected by the disease of his boredom?

The Reflections of One Hearer

Another great British layman of the Noncomformist heritage
was Bernard Lord Manning, senior tutor of Jesus College, Cam-
bridge. He also wrote helpful books on spiritual themes and in
one he includes an address, given to the students at a theological college, entitled "Effectual Preaching: The Reflexions
of One Hearer". Lord Manning told the theologues that he came
before them not as an instructor but as a reporter, who brought
tidings from the back pew where he had sat twice every Sunday
for more years than he could remember. Reminding them of the
centrality of preaching in the Reformed Church tradition, he singled out as the first and absolutely essential condition of effectual
preaching that it must be interesting. He said, "If people are
bored you might as well be silent. Not only will you not help
your hearers, you will soon have no hearers." He added this barb
– "Do not fancy that your predecessors have reduced your congregation to its irreducable minimum." From the many features
of a dull sermon Manning singled out theological jargon which
may have its place in the class-room but which is totally unintel-
ligible to the average congregation. He deplored the use of such
terms as "cosmic significance", "scientific method", "ultimate
reality", "relative truth", and the sophisticated reference to the

Second Isaiah or the Pastoral Epistles or the Synoptic Gospels – which preachers bring into the pulpit only because they are too lazy to translate them into intelligible language. Himself a scholar, Lord Manning believed that there should be scholarship behind every sermon, but it should be an implicit scholarship and not the kind that "parades itself and is merely boring to plain men". He said, "Make your scholarship really your own, an inextricable part of your own minds, so that it emerges unconsciously and unnoticed, and is not flung out in profitless and undigested lumps." Lord Manning closed with a word about pulpit demeanour, warning the students that they must not expect a sermon to interest the congregation unless the preacher himself is obviously interested by it. He said, "Sometimes you talk as if you have nothing very urgent to say, nothing that demanded very serious attention, nothing that moved you very much and nothing that greatly mattered to us. You may believe that it matters, but no one would think so."[5]

Despite the pessimism of certain critics, I believe that the level of preaching across the Church today is generally rather high. To be sure, we may not be producing the pulpit giants of former years, and some of our great metropolitan preaching centres may have difficulty finding star performers, but the layman who travels through the cities and towns and villages of the land can worship in any church and, if he makes the effort to listen, be certain of hearing a sermon that will stimulate his mind and feed his soul. Unfortunately, however, the layman may *have* to make an effort to listen, simply because so many preachers do not make the effort to be interesting. On Sunday mornings they serve a substantial diet of theological food but, perhaps because of other demands made on their time during the week, they serve it like a cake which has been removed from the oven half-baked. Such men really do not preach at all; they think aloud in the pulpit. Their sermons have not been worked out and thoroughly prepared; they are not ready to be served to the congregation.

We must keep reminding ourselves that we live in days when television has conditioned people to professional standards in all forms of communication. Consider the amount of preparation that goes into a half-hour television show – the writing and re-writing of the script, the endless rehearsals, the precise timing, the effort to achieve sequence and climactic effect. The programme has to be perfected, because the listener, if it bores him, can switch the dial to another channel; and the great aim of the producer is to keep him rooted in his armchair. The worshipper also can turn a dial, either by closing his mind to the sound that comes from the pulpit or by absenting himself from worship altogether. We preachers cannot compel our audiences to listen to the Gospel but, if we do want them to listen, we must give our messages audience-appeal. A quality of showmanship characterises the best sermons. Despise it, if you will, and accuse the preacher of "hamming it up". It is true that some men have mastered the art of saying nothing exquisitely, but it is also true, as Paul said, that if you speak uninterestingly and fail to command the attention of your congregation you will be talking into the air.

Ten Marks of an Interesting Sermon

One of the Yale lecturers, whose name eludes me, made a wise suggestion. He advised the minister to sit in a pew of his own church on Saturday evening and think through the sermon which he has prepared for the following day. Let him identify himself with his people and let him honestly ask himself, "Would this sermon interest me? Would it speak to my needs? Would it grip and hold my attention if someone else were going to preach it?" Suppose in our imagination we follow that advice? Suppose we listen to ourselves preach? What in our judgment are some of the qualities essential in a sermon to make it interesting?

1. *An arresting introduction.* The opening sentences will not slide into the subject like a tired tombstone but will attack it with a trumpet note of originality. By proclaiming immediately the urgency of the subject and by putting the listener into the picture they will compel him to sit up and take notice.

2. *A logical sequence of thought.* From the very opening sentence it will be clear that the preacher is in control of his subject – and of his congregation. He knows where he is going and he intends to take his listeners with him. By organising his material carefully he makes it possible for the congregation to keep up

with him and follow his train of thought. The sermon is well-structured, though the bones are not protruding from its flesh.

3. *Picturesque language.* The preacher will clothe his ideas in concrete words and phrases which have been chiselled and polished like a finely wrought piece of sculpture. He will paint pictures that remain fixed in the mind. He will speak in simple language, the only language that men understand and to which they respond. The battle of Trafalgar would not have been won if Nelson's "England expects that every man will do his duty" had read, "The U.K. anticipates as regards the current emergency that personnel will face up to the issues involved and exercise all the functions allotted to their respective occupation groups".

4. *Literary skills.* The sermon will possess literary excellence – not to focus attention on itself or to usurp the glory that belongs only to Christ but to be as worthy a vehicle as possible for mediating Christ. Similes, alliteration and metaphors are not gimmicks; they are legitimate literary devices utilised by great orators like Sir Winston Churchill whose public utterances captured the attention and still live in the memory of all who heard them.

5. *Good illustrations.* They will not be the old chestnuts nor will they try to compensate for the preacher's own poverty of thought. Carefully chosen, sparingly used and strategically placed, they will be fresh and surprising. They will be taken from history, poetry, biography, drama, journalism, science and from the preacher's own experience. They will effectively clinch his arguments, lighting up the truth of his discourse and making it applicable to real life.

6. *Dramatic presentation.* There will be an element of drama in a sermon with audience-appeal, a variety of moods, a subtle interplay of climax and anti-climax. How can it be otherwise? The preacher is supposed to be talking about a drama, God's great drama of redemption. He can scarcely command a hearing if he sounds as though he were reciting the weather forecast or reading the minutes of the last meeting. He will try to dramatise the Gospel with at least as much enthusiasm as some radio hucksters dramatise deodorants and beer.

7. *Sense of humour.* There is humour in a good sermon – not

jokes that draw belly-laughs or make people blush, but a subtle use of comic relief that relaxes the tension and enables the preacher to say some serious things without giving offence. Pomposity in the pulpit gets people's backs up, solemnity bores them, and stuffiness they switch off. Yet a congregation will swallow some bitter pills when they are coated in the sugar of good humour.

8. *Pleasing delivery.* The sermon will not be read but preached. The preacher will look directly into the faces of his congregation – an eyeball-to-eyeball confrontation. He will preach with skill of a violinist playing a concerto, changing his tempo, varying his voice, sinking at times to a whisper and rising to controlled crescendos.

9. *Appeal to the whole personality.* The sermon will involve the listener as a whole person. It will impart information that stimulates his mind and doesn't simply tell him what he already knows. It will play a tune on the strings of his heart, bringing tears to his eyes and a smile to his lips. If he is a normal person he would rather be moved than bored.

10. *A challenging conclusion.* When the sermon is finished, there will be no need to ask, "What was it all about?" Its purpose will be plain. Nor will the listener be tempted to retort, "Oh Yeah!" or "So What?" He will know that God has spoken to him through the preacher's word, challenging him to a renewed dedication and obedience.

RELEVANT TO CONGREGATION

Having lunch together after attending a Sunday morning service, two laymen conducted a post-mortem on the sermon. Both expressed admiration for the preacher's eloquence and for the theological soundness of his discourse, but something seemed lacking in its quality, and neither could put his finger on it. At last, as they were having their coffee, one man burst out, "I know what bothered me about that sermon – it could have been preached a hundred years ago."

It is a profitable discipline to study the hundred-year-old sermons of the great pulpit masters of past generations – Robertson, Newman, Jowett, Beecher, Phillips Brooks and others. They teach us a great deal about the craft of preaching. They possess a timeless quality in that they proclaim the everlasting Gospel and convey eternal truths that never change, but we dare not plagiarise them, because they are so obviously dated. They don't speak to the specific needs of people in the second half of the twentieth century. To have audience-appeal now, so that it becomes a joint enterprise of the preacher and his hearers, a sermon must not only be suited and interesting to the congregation; it must be relevant to the congregation. It must be timely, cogent and contemporaneous.

Most preachers have learned by experience that the sermons to which people listen and respond are those which encounter them where they are and speak directly to the needs and problems of their lives. That is why the spokesman for God will steep himself not only in the Bible and theological literature but in everything which comprises what we call our "culture", man's own interpretation of his contemporary situation. He will read the newspapers, the periodicals, the latest works of fiction, the popular plays, and even expose himself to the vibrations of modern rock and the exclamations of modern art. These facets of culture may not give the right answers but they may be asking the right questions, and sometimes we come closer to the truth in great questions than in small answers. It angered the suffering Job that his smug "comforters" gave such small answers to his great questions. Their constricted, outdated religious orthodoxy did not come to terms with the facts; and he, Job, sitting on his dunghill and scraping his boils, was one of those facts. There are certain facts in the human situation today which preachers cannot ignore; and our presentation of the Gospel, if it would be relevant, must squarely face up to them.

Change

The most imperious new fact in the present situation is change. A few years ago the students in a mid-west theological seminary staged a brilliantly communicative musical revue called *Sure as You're Born*. One scene showed the interior of a typical suburban church. The minister, Donald Greene, stands in the pulpit. Across from him sitting alone on a single row of chairs is Peter

Evans, the Chairman of the Board (spell "bored" in two ways). Their relationship has not been harmonious. They have no mutual rapport. Both of them air their grievances. Evans complains about the muddled theology of most preachers. "Talk about confusion," he sings. Greene answers by posing the big problem that faces him: "How do you preach in an age that's changing?" That is precisely the preacher's problem, and he will not solve it by pretending that it does not exist. The truth is that we who were born during the past fifty years have been caught up in the most rapid changes in mankind's history. Within this brief period the human situation has changed more radically and more frequently than in all the centuries betwen the coming of Christ and the middle of the last century. We don't have to dream of revolutions anymore. We are living in one. Scientifically, politically, economically, culturally and sexually, the world is in a state of flux. It is like a kaleidescope, its pattern likely to change overnight. How do you convince people that God plays a part in this age of revolution? How do you help them to see revolution as the activity of God and to discern a divine purpose running through the rapidly changing events of our day? How do you preach in an age that's changing?

Technology

Another fact which the preacher cannot ignore is the unprecedented challenge to the Gospel which is determined and dominated by the rise of modern science and the growth of technology. Professor Herbert Butterfield, himself a believing Christian, declares that the scientific revolution "outshines everything since the rise of Christianity and reduces the Renaissance and Reformation to the rank of mere episodes, mere internal displacements within the system of medieval Christendom . . ." The Church today lives in a totally new situation. The one supreme fact with which it must reckon is the advent of a new way of thinking and a new way of living brought to pass through a changing conception of life and the universe and through man's increasing mastery over physical nature. The principal feature of this new way of thinking is man's belief that he can use his increasing knowledge and technical skill to shape his environment, his society, himself and his own destiny. When Professor Morris Ginsberg was one of the Presidents of the British Association he wrote an obituary on all ideologies. He said that there are no ideologies left in the world now except the ideology of science which he defined as "the passionate conviction that science can solve all social problems and that science means empirically verifiable knowledge." Any minister who preaches the Gospel today without reckoning that the Gospel is challenged by the impact on men's minds of the scientific revolution and its attendant philosophy of self-salvation will simply be talking into the air.

Affluence

The changes brought about by science and technology have given birth to another new factor in the human situation – affluence. Every preacher owes it to himself to read J. K. Galbraith's book *The Affluent Society*.[6] Galbraith begins by reminding us that throughout history nearly all peoples have been very poor and have taken their poverty for granted. Poverty was the all-pervasive fact of their lives. Poverty is still the all-pervasive fact of many lives, but not the lives of people who ordinarily listen to sermons. In the last few generations, in Europe and more especially in North America, there has been a great and quite unprecedented affluence. One newspaper recently listed a number of things which are not even considered status symbols any more: the outdoor barbecue pit, the mink stole, the stereo set, the do-it-yourself project, the rumpus room, the new house, the outdoor swimming-pool. Most of these things are now so common that they are no longer hallmarks of distinction, and the list grows longer every year. Yet, as Galbraith makes very clear, the ideas by which people in this favoured part of the world interpret their existence and in some measure guide their behaviour were not forged in a world of wealth; they were the product of a world in which poverty had always been man's normal lot and in which any other state seemed unimaginable. The question to be asked now is whether we can still be guided, even in part, by virtues and ideas that were relevant to a previous age. We know that much of the New Testament is addressed to poverty, slavery and hunger and that it has a great deal to say to the underprivileged

49

members of society. Do we know also that much of the New Testament, especially the teaching of Jesus, is addressed to prosperity, freedom and affluence and that it says some direct things to the strong, successful, self-reliant members of society? How shall we say them now? How shall we dispense the Bread of Life to people with five-figure incomes and a suburban bungalow and two cars in the garage and a country home and hospitals and schools and charities and state benefits and amusements that seem to fill their lives with ample meaning? The preacher will have to figure that one out if he wants to be relevant.

Fear

The preacher who wants to be relevant to his congregation must also take account of the fact that, despite all our affluence and scientific prowess, we live in a world where the prevailing mood is one of fear. To be sure, a few million people have risen above poverty, but it only heightens the wall that alienates them from three-quarters of the world's population who live in deepest poverty. The linking of continents by satellites and jet aeroplanes has done nothing to link the hearts of men in human brotherhood. The footsteps of men on the surface of the moon have changed none of the ground rules on the surface of earth. We could continue interminably with our dreary recital of clever contrasts, but it all adds up to this: The prevailing fact in people's lives is not the enjoyment of their shiny new gadgets but the fear that these shiny new gadgets will be violently taken from them or an- nihilated in a hydrogen blast. A man's life does not consist in the abundance of his possessions when he has to defend them with the use of firearms, and a woman's life is more than clothing when she cannot walk the streets in safety at night. Professor G. M. Carstairs of Edinburgh University said in a public lecture that fear is the great threat to mental health in our generation. He catalogued some genuine fears of which the first and most obvious is the fear of the bomb. He said, "We live in a world where the lunatic dialogue of 'if you blow me up I will blow you up' has become a serious reality. Our children are living in a folklore of bombs." No pulpit platitudes will mitigate that reality. Our young people, if they still pay attention to the pulpit, want to know how a folklore of bombs fits into the providence of God; they want to know how to live in this new and frightening age.

Minority

What makes it so difficult for the preacher to speak relevantly to a situation dominated by the foregoing facts is the additional fact stated by Peter Berger in his book, *A Rumour of Angels.*[1] He says, "There is strong evidence that traditional religious beliefs have become empty of meaning, not only in large sections of the general population but even among many people who, with whatever motives, continue to belong to a church." (Page 6) Many sermons today run smack into the stone wall of empty pews because preachers do not realise or will not accept the fact that the dimension of the Supernatural has largely disappeared, not only from the minds of people outside the Church but from the minds of many people who might otherwise be inside the Church. In other words, they have ceased to believe in God. Berger says, "This means that those to whom the supernatural is still, or again, a meaningful reality find themselves in the status of a minority, more precisely a cognitive minority." (Page 7) He goes on to say, "The status of a cognitive minority is thus invariably an uncomfortable one – not necessarily because the majority is repressive or intolerant, but simply because it refuses to accept the minority's definition of reality as 'knowledge'." (Page 8) Where does that put the preacher? Where does it put the Bible? Where does it put the Apostles' Creed? Where does it put the faith once delivered to the saints? A theological crisis exists today, a widening gulf between pulpit and pew; and the preacher will not bridge it with a neo-dogmatism that only superficially covers an underlying sense of panic.

Beyond the Fringe

You will have a good laugh if you listen to the recording of the English satirical revue, produced on Broadway, called *Beyond the Fringe.* One of the characters wearing a clerical collar does a burlesque of a sermon. In a pompous, parsonic, unctuous tone he speaks for ten minutes and says absolutely nothing. He quotes a meaningless text – "But my brother Esau is an hairy man but I am a smooth man", and never returns to it until the last sentence. He takes an obsequious approach – "words we might do very much worse than to consider"; drags in the old clichés – "as I was on my way here tonight"; uses stuffy phrases – "an employee of the railway company hailed me"; speaks condescendingly – "very many years ago when I was about as old as some of you are now"; uses trite illustrations – "life, you know, is rather like a tin of sardines"; resorts to ludicrous colloquialisms – "stuff that for a lark"; and ends with the usual platitudes – "and so now I draw to a close, I want you to go out into the world . . ."

On the night when I saw the revue in London the audience split its sides laughing. I also laughed at first, then I began to squirm uncomfortably. Was that an actor up on the stage or was it a caricature of me? The sermon had inverted audience-appeal. The theatre-goers, who may once have been church-goers, responded hilariously, because that was exactly how they thought of sermons. It is exactly how a great many people think of sermons and it could be one of the reasons they no longer respond to sermons or even listen to them any more.

CHAPTER NOTES

1   T. E. Jessop, *Effective Religion* (Whitehead, London, 1944), pp. 30–31.
2   Marian Anderson, *My Lord, What a Morning* (Cresset Press, London, 1957), p. 188.
3   Ibid.
4   Halford Luccock, *Communicating the Gospel* (Harper, New York, 1954), pp. 47–48.
5   Bernard Lord Manning, M.A., *A Layman in the Ministry* (Independent Press, London, 1942), pp. 135–9.
6   Penguin Books, London, 1958.
7   Doubleday, Garden City, N.Y., 1969.

CHAPTER THREE

Great Themes for Great Times

Why People are Leaving the Churches

If some preachers today are losing their congregations, it could be a judgment upon them for losing the Word of God. In a searching article published in *Religion and Life* Donald G. Bloesch attributes the increasing number of empty pews to a type of preaching which is not proclamation of the Word of God but proclamation of a secularised theology that lacks spiritual authority and power. He believes that people are leaving the churches because preachers are driving them away. He fears that Protestantism, which was born out of a rediscovery of the sermon, is in danger of forfeiting its heritage. He gives as the reason the fact that many sermons today appeal more to the social sciences than to Scripture. Moral and sometimes political lectures have taken the place of Gospel proclamation, and laymen are not interested in listening to them. Dr. Bloesch concludes his article by saying

"It is not in itself a disaster that many people are withdrawing from the churches. Emil Brunner has said that what are needed are ministers who will drive people out of the church by the preaching of the biblical gospel which is a stumbling block to Jews and folly to Greeks. The trouble today is that people are being alienated from the church not by the scandal of the Cross but by false stumbling blocks such as the union of religion and a welfare state ideology."[1]

Perhaps the same situation accounts at least partly for the exodus of ministers from the churches. Undoubtedly a host of external factors have caused a crisis in the Church's ministry today, but that crisis is minimal compared to the crisis of conscience in many ministers themselves. A minister knows that he is supposed to be God's spokesman. He knows that the pulpit is holy ground. The Church ordained him to preach the Word of God, not simply to express his own opinions. If he has nothing theological to say, he has nothing to say; and there comes a time, if he is honest with himself, when he admits that to remain in the pulpit would be an act of sheer exploitation and blasphemy.

Such was the discovery of D. R. Davies, a former Congregational minister in Britain, whose spiritual autobiography, *In Search of Myself*, every preacher ought to read because he will see a reflection of his own hypocrisy in the author's relentless self-analysis. Davies with utmost candour confesses that what put him at odds with his congregation and drove him out of the ministry was the uncomfortable awareness that he did not have a Gospel to preach. He had only a secular humanism, a naive confidence in man's capacity to be inherently good and love his neighbour and build the Kingdom of God on earth. In fact, he despised what he called "the morbid deviations of theological orthodoxy" which overlay New Testament Christianity. He deplored "the classic concentration on sin" which obscured "the original, sunny, simple teaching of Jesus". He believed that nothing mattered but the principle of love and its out-working in the structure of social institutions. Therefore, he preached on all sorts of topics – pacifism, education, labour relations, state welfare, etc. He also emptied the pews of his church. Many years later, after a spiritual pilgrimage that took him down every avenue of religious and political belief, ending in anarchy and atheism, he said, "I realise only too well how 'the hungry sheep looked up and were not fed'. I gave them ideas, but no Gospel."[2]

Paul's Sermon

Among the many phrases in our modern church jargon which I should like to bury for a while is the outworn phrase

54

"communicating the Gospel". It comes at us from every angle, both from the critics outside the Church and from experts inside the Church, as though the all-important thing about the Christian message were the technique of getting it across. Surely, however, it matters not so much *how* we communicate as *what* we communicate, not so much how we shall preach our sermons as whether they are worth preaching. By all means let us use and perfect every technique of communicating the Gospel, provided it is the *Gospel* we are communicating and not some sterile humanistic aberration which has no power to re-create and redeem.

Let it be frankly admitted that in terms of techniques the Apostle Paul may not always have attained first-class honours as a preacher. At least, such seems the case with his efforts to communicate the Gospel on Mars Hill in the city of Athens. It was probably the driest sermon that he ever preached and might be criticised from many angles. To begin with, it was far too sophisticated even for a congregation of eggheads who, despite their intellectual veneer, may have cried out from the hunger of their souls. It was too brief and concise and moved too quickly, burying the listeners under an avalanche of Christian concepts which were as foreign to them as to a congregation of illiterate peasants. Moreover, Paul spoke too ingratiatingly, almost apologising for his message instead of presenting it with his usual clarity and forthrightness. All this we can say about Paul's sermon on Mars Hill, but one thing we cannot say: we cannot accuse Paul of failing to preach the Gospel. Homiletically sound or not, his brief discourse set forth the whole truth of God's revelation in Christ. Actually it was a great sermon, one of the greatest ever preached; and if we read, mark, learn and inwardly digest it, we shall see that it contained everything essential to a full proclamation of the Christian Gospel:

So Paul, standing in the middle of the Areopagus, said: "Men of Athens, I perceive that in every way you are very religious. For as I passed along, and observed the objects of your worship, I found also an altar with this inscription, 'To an unknown god.' What therefore you worship as unknown, this I proclaim to you. The God who made the world and everything in it, being Lord of heaven and earth, does not live in shrines made by man, nor is he served by human hands, as though he needed anything, since he himself gives to all men life and breath and everything. And he made from one every nation of men to live on all the face of the earth, having determined allotted periods and the boundaries of their habitation, that they should seek God, in the hope that they might feel after him and find him. Yet he is not far from each one of us, for 'In him we live and move and have our being'; as even some of your poets have said, 'For we are indeed his offspring.' Being then God's offspring, we ought not to think that the Deity is like gold, or silver, or stone, a representation by the art and imagination of man. The times of ignorance God overlooked, but now he commands all men everywhere to repent, because he has fixed a day on which he will judge the world in righteousness by a man whom he has appointed, and of this he has given assurance to all men by raising him from the dead." (Acts 17:22-31 R.S.V.)

When I became the minister of Chalmers United Church, Ottawa, I succeeded Dr. John Woodside, a giant of a man who in his retirement proved to be a gracious and kindly father-in-God. Rarely did he presume to advise me, much as I needed and sought his advice. Once he did say, "Don't neglect your preaching. Whatever the demands on your time and energy, always give sermon preparation the first priority. Your people will forgive you all else if you maintain a high standard of pulpit ministry, but nothing else you can do for them will compensate for failure in the pulpit." Again he said, "Stick to the great themes. You have no time to waste on trivialities. If God spared you to preach twice a week for the next forty years, you could never exhaust the great themes." Then he added, "What matters each Sunday is not that people shall say, 'Isn't he a great preacher?' or 'Wasn't that a great sermon?', but that they shall say, 'Isn't it a great Gospel?' "

That is what we have to say about the sermon that Paul preached in Athens. To be sure, most of the congregation reacted indifferently – due partly to their own spiritual deficiencies and partly to the fact that the message lacked audience-appeal. Like an over-weighted aeroplane it never left the ground. Yet the astonishing thing is that after two thousand years it still lives and men still read it, finding it a means of grace that enlightens their minds and binds them to God. The reason is that, despite any homiletical shortcomings, Paul on Mars Hill preached the great themes of the gospel, the greatest the Athenians had ever heard; and whether our congregations recognise it or not, these are the themes that speak most directly to the human situation today.

GOD

Paul on Mars Hill spoke to his congregation an authentic word about God. That should be the starting-point for any preacher who dares to stand in the prophetic tradition. The laymen in the pews know more than he knows about literature and history and psychology and politics and economics. They may be experts in those secular subjects and, if they are experts, they come to Church expecting to hear a man who himself is an expert on the Bible and on what the Bible tells us about God. As Karl Barth has written, "In the Church of Jesus Christ men speak about God and come to hear about God. About God the Father, the Son and the Holy Spirit; about God's grace and truth; about God's thoughts and works; about God's promises, ordinances and commandments; about God's kingdom, and about the state and life of man in the sphere of his lordship. But always and in all circumstances about God himself, who is the presupposition, meaning and power of everything that is to be said and heard in the Church . . ."[3] God is the preacher's subject. The preacher has something to say about God, something to say from God, or he has nothing to say at all.

God Makes the Headlines

It is a pity that John A. T. Robinson (formerly the Bishop of Woolwich) should be identified almost exclusively with his controversial book, *Honest to God*, because it diverts attention from his more mature, original and important writings. In his later book, *Exploration into God*,[4] he reminds us that there are fashions in theology like everything else and he gives us a thumbnail sketch of the history of those fashions over the past fifty years. In the 1920s and early 30s the Church, under the impact of historical criticism and liberal theology, was chiefly concerned with the doctrine of the Person of Christ. In the late 30s and 40s, under the menacing cloud of strange and rival ideologies, attention had become focused on the doctrine of Man. In the early 50s, amid the anxieties of a nuclear age and guided by the theme of the Evanston Assembly, "Jesus Christ the Hope of the World", men's minds turned to eschatology, the doctrine of the End. When the World Council met again at New Delhi in 1961, the focus of ferment and renewal was the doctrine of the Church itself. And now, says Dr. Robinson, "we are agitated, most deeply of all, by a thorough-going reappraisal of the doctrine of *God*."

He points out this important difference, however. Whereas the previous debates took place within the Church, which is usually interested in matters of theology, the debate about God has broken through the Church and become the concern of people outside. Today God is the subject not only of preachers but of novelists, dramatists, film producers, actors, poets, philosophers, psychiatrists and newspaper columnists. Today we read articles about God not only in the religious press but in the secular press. God has become news. Indeed, so much publicity attended the debut of *Honest to God* and the debate which it sparked off that I entitled a subsequent sermon, "God Makes the Headlines", which itself was quoted in several newspapers throughout Great Britain. Even atheists cannot leave the subject of God alone. God fascinates them as a candle fascinates a moth. Some broadcasters, who profess to be atheists, seem almost to have an obsession with God. They talk more about God than do preachers and Church assemblies which express themselves authoritatively on every subject of moral, political and social concern but rarely say anything about God. Someone has observed that God may be dead, but he is also and most certainly making the scene.

A few years ago, when I was minister of the City Temple and looking for ways of communicating the Christian message, I managed to get an interview with the most powerful publisher in

Britain. He had his office high up in the building next to mine, so he looked down on the church from a great height – in more ways than one. "Why do you want to write for my newspaper?" he barked. "Do you think it will fill your church? Nothing will fill your church or any other church ever again! The churches in this country are dead! The Established Church is dead! The Free Churches are deader!" He added, "Don't tell me about church-going in North America. It doesn't mean a thing!" After getting these strictures off his chest, he mellowed slightly. Seizing the opportunity, I asked him, "You who are so closely attuned to public opinion, what do you think that people want the Church to tell them?" I expected that he would say something about the bomb or sex or race prejudice, but to my surprise he made no reference to moral and social questions at all. He seemed to imply that on these issues piety is no substitute for competence and that other voices speak more knowledgeably and authoritatively than the voice of the Church. "The Church's business," he said, "is to talk about God. People are sceptical these days and they need to be assured that there is a God. They want to know what God is like and what he is doing."

Questions People Ask

In spite of all the publicity that God is getting, there are still a great many people who need to be convinced that he exists. Some are outright atheists, dogmatic in their doubts and receiving more attention in the magazines and on television than they deserve. Others are honest agnostics, and agnosticism can be an agonising frame of mind, as seen in modern plays and novels where characters cry passionately for some ultimate truth that will solve the senseless riddle of human existence. Others have a more basic need. They are indifferent to God, they don't care enough to disbelieve in him, they don't even think of God or reckon with him as a live factor in human experience. The Bible will not convince them because the Bible does not attempt to prove the reality of God; it takes God for granted just as a biography of Napoleon takes the existence of Napoleon for granted. Nor will sermons have any effect upon them, because they no longer listen to sermons. Nevertheless, the Bible does speak directly to these modern pagans, if its message could somehow be communicated so as to penetrate their closed minds. They need to hear the Word of Isaiah (Chap. 28) which lashed like a whip the drunken magnates of Jerusalem. "Men may try to ignore God," he thundered, "but God will not be ignored. God speaks twice to men, both times very simply and plainly. If they refuse to hear his words they must listen to his voice in events." The situation has not changed. Men still need to be told that, in bowing God out of his own world, they have dismissed the author and director of the human drama without whose direction the drama can only degenerate into a colossal farce.

Church people may not need to be convinced that there is a God, but it certainly rests upon the pulpit to tell them what God is like and in this regard to correct some of their mistaken ideas. On the one hand, there are those who still think of God as the vague impersonal Life Force of the philosophers, a Supreme Being, remote from his world, uninvolved in its affairs, whose existence need not affect us in the way we live. On the other hand, there are those who familiarise God, reducing him to what someone has called "a celestial chore-boy loafing around his universe and pitifully pleading to be made use of". Popular songs used to rhapsodise him as the "Regular Good Guy" and the "Man Upstairs". One voluptuous Hollywood actress described him as a "Livin' Doll". We shall correct those mistaken ideas by nothing less than a consistent and faithful proclamation of the great doctrines of the Faith, especially the Doctrine of the Incarnation. Let us begin always by insisting that the Incarnation is primarily a truth not about the divinity of Christ but about the character of God. We do not apply to Jesus our preconceived ideas about God; rather we look first at Jesus and from him learn everything that we know with any certainty about God. No one ever described the winsome but stern man of the Gospels as an Impersonal Life Force or a Livin' Doll. He who entered this world in a manger of humiliation, who identified himself with human need and treated sin so seriously that he died on a cross to forgive it, is neither an Impersonal Life Force nor a celestial chore-boy. He is a God very close to us, his life inescapably and inextricably bound up with ours, and he compels us to reckon with him on his own terms.

It is not enough, however, to tell our people what God is like and what he has done, because even the most staunch Christians, unconsciously perhaps, ask a more burning question of the pulpit. They want to know what God is doing now. Do we ourselves not feel haunted by that query as we contemplate the tragedy of our world, the injustices of human life, the spectacle of innocent suffering, the discouragements and defeats that crush us in our work? We ask, "Where is God? What on earth is he doing?" Here we may speak with confidence from "the strange world of the Bible", for the Bible is the story of God's activity in human history and human life. We read the Book of Exodus, not as a history of the Jews but as a chronicle of God's dealings with his people in every generation – seeing their sufferings, redeeming them in his own way, manifesting his power, leading them through the wilderness and demanding their trust and obedience. Second Isaiah provides a clear insight into the workings of God, revealing him not as an external factor who needs to be propitiated and brought to bear upon the human situation, but as an internal factor already at work within the human situation, controlling it and making even the wrath of men to praise him. Nothing speaks more directly to the individual about the role that God plays in his life than do the familiar Psalms – the twenty-third Psalm showing him as a God who cares; the thirty-eighth, a God who chastens; the fifty-first, a God who pardons; the fifty-fifth, a God who supports; the ninety-first, a God who protects; the hundred and seventh, a God who rescues; the hundred and thirty-ninth, a God who pursues.[5] Again we must proclaim the great doctrines of our Faith, especially the Doctrine of the Trinity, for we have not said everything that we know about God until we have shown that the Father above us who has revealed himself in the Son beside us is also the Holy Spirit working within and among us as the most real factor in life and history.

The most classic sermon about God ever preached was Paul's sermon to the Greek philosophers on Mars Hill. Homiletically sound or not, it contained the great biblical truths about God: his Creatorhood – the truth that he made all things out of nothing; God's Sovereignty – the truth that he determined and administers the natural and moral laws of the universe; God's Transcendence – the truth that he is the wholly Other who cannot be contained in man's philosophies or institutions; God's Immanence – the truth that he does not exist outside creation but that all creation exists within him. These are the great themes about God, the basic tenets of the Christian Faith. These are the themes that people expect to hear from a preacher if and when they come to church; and it is certain that, if they don't hear them, they will eventually and with good reason stop coming to church.

MAN
What is Man?

Next, Paul on Mars Hill spoke to his congregation an authentic word about Man. In ages past, when space travel was science fiction and not a common-place occurrence, I read a story about four astronauts who landed on another planet. Disembarking from their spacecraft they were confronted by a group of scaly little creatures who by strange coincidence not only communicated through spoken language but happened to speak English. One of them stepped forward and addressed the chief astronaut. "What are you?" he asked. "I am a man," came the reply. The scaly little creature looked more puzzled than ever. "And what," he inquired, "is a man?"

It was a fundamental question. Unfortunately I cannot recall what answer the astronaut gave, but it doesn't matter. What does matter is the answer that *we* give and the answer given by our society. Upon our definition of man, our view of the nature and destiny of man, all the practical issues of life hang – our solution to the great social problems of race, crime, poverty and war, as well as the more personal decisions affecting our own lives.

What is man? From all directions – science, psychology, politics, industry – come the world's answers to that eternal question, and we could make them a very absorbing comparative study. As preachers it is our business to tell people what the Bible thinks of man, and from the "strange world of the Bible" to correct two diametrically opposite misconceptions. There are voices in our mechanised civilisation that *debunk* man, pulverise his soul and reduce his personality from one to zero. Someone has observed that on the one hand we have learned to make machines so much like men in their behaviour that they seem almost human, while on the other hand humans are in many respects beginning to act like machines. Then there are the voices that *deify* man and urge him to think of himself as God. They tell him that he came into existence by biological accident, that his thinking simply represents a higher form of evolution, that his idols are only the projection of his ideals, that morality is a composition of his own values and that his destiny will be entirely what he makes of it.

The Bible View of Man

Paul's sermon on Mars Hill speaks to both of these misconceptions. It begins by emphasising the truth of man's creaturehood; and that is where every sermon needs to begin. Man is a creature. He did not bring himself into existence. Man exists by the creative power, within the providence and under the sovereignty of Almighty God. Nor is it a denial of man's dignity to accept his rightful status as a creature and acknowledge his dependence upon God; rather it will give him a dignity that he could never give himself. The doghood of a dog is in the dog, but the manhood of a man is not in the man; it is in his relationship to God. When he breaks that relationship he loses something of his manhood. Man is a creature; he is not God. If he tries to make himself God he will not rise above his station but will fall below it; he will become something less than God created him, something sub-human and chaotic.

Yet we have not spoken the whole truth about man by describing him as a creature, because man differs from all other creatures not only in degree but in kind. Man is a child of God. Let him look at himself in the mirror of the Bible. Let him ponder the meaning of the words, "God made man in his own image." Let him steep his mind in the thought of an Old Testament psalmist who could contemplate the vastness and variety of the stellar universe and yet marvel that God, whose creative power brought the worlds into being, does for him what he does not do for all the planets and solar systems – he is mindful of him and visits him, he loves him with an everlasting love (Psalm 8). Let man steep his mind in the teachings of Jesus who declared that the whole world cannot be set in the balance over against one human soul. Not only does God value man more highly than the rest of creation. Like a shepherd, who leaves his flock while he seeks for a single stray, God leaves the whole universe to run itself while he seeks the salvation of one human soul.

"God made man in his own image." We should be less than realistic if we failed to take account of the distortion of that image in man's nature. The Bible takes account of it. The Bible sees man as a child of God, but as a fallen child of God, a sinner. Perhaps we have glossed over the doctrine of the Fall of Man, because as a doctrine it is traditionally associated with the Old Testament story of Adam and Eve. Some people do not believe that story; they explain it away as a myth and think that they have thereby explained away the truth which it communicates. The Fall of Man is neither a myth nor a doctrine but a fact which the very confusion of people's lives and the ghastly predicament of our world should make distressingly evident. We grasp its truth only when we see how far we have fallen, and that becomes plain not in the Old Testament where the doctrine originates but in the New Testament where we can see the measure of manhood in Jesus. Jesus came not only to reveal God; he came to reveal man, essential man as God created him and as God intended him to be. Jesus is the measure of manhood, the true dignity and the full stature of human nature in the image of God. We look at him and learn what it means to be human, mature, full-grown and perfect. We look at ourselves and we know that compared with him we are not men at all but sub-men who have fallen far below the level of true human nature.

That is why the preacher must always lead his people to the Cross where man learns the final truth about himself – that he is a creature, a child of God, a fallen child, but also a child for whom Christ died. There are two factors in the Cross of Christ: a life lived without sin, with faith unshaken and with unfaltering love; and a concentration of human wickedness that violently assaulted that life and tried to destroy it. Calvary was the decisive conflict between man and sub-man. On Calvary the eternal God once and for all dealt with the terrible fact of human sin. It was his way of reversing the Fall, of meeting us where we

are so that he could raise us again to our full stature as Sons
of God and restore the image which by our sin we had de-
faced. The Cross does not simply lay a moral obligation on us;
it changes our status as human beings. It makes us men for whom
Christ died – sinners, to be sure, but redeemed sinners.

JUDGMENT
The Uncomfortable Pulpit
   A Canadian journalist and broadcaster wrote a book called *The
Comfortable Pew*,[6] an indictment of the Church which mainly
created the impression that the author had not been in many
church pews, otherwise he would have known that even in a material sense pews are notoriously uncomfortable, especially toward
the close of a lengthy sermon. It was even more evident that he
had not been inside many pulpits, else he would have known that
the pulpit can be the most uncomfortable place in the world, especially if God gives the preacher a Word of Judgment to proclaim.
   Paul on Mars Hill spoke to his congregation a Word of God's
Judgment: "God ... commands all men everywhere to repent,
because he has fixed a day on which he will judge the world in
righteousness by a man whom he has appointed...." That may
have been the point where the Greek philosophers grew rest-
less and ceased to listen sympathetically. Perhaps the whole idea
of judgment scared them off. It scared off Felix the Roman Gov-
ernor who, when Paul preached to him about the coming judgment, became alarmed and exclaimed "That will do for the present; when I find it convenient I will send for you again" (Acts
24:24-25). The Gospel of Judgment still scares people off.
   Early in his career a minister has to make a decision. Will he
speak the truth as God gives it to him or will he speak only the
soothing words that people like to hear? Will he preach the Gospel or will he preach what J. K. Galbraith[7] calls the "conventional wisdom", viz., that which people can best understand, that
which they find most acceptable and that which contributes to
their self-esteem? Galbraith writes:

   "The hallmark of the conventional wisdom is acceptability. It has the approval of those to whom it is addressed. There are many reasons why people like to hear articulated that which they approve. It serves the ego: the individual has the satisfaction of knowing that other and more famous people share his conclusions. To hear what he believes is also a source of reassurance. The individual knows that he is supported in his thoughts – that he has not been left behind and alone. Further, to hear what one approves serves the evangelising instinct. It means that others are also hearing and are thereby in the process of being persuaded."

Galbraith could be writing about some preachers when he goes on to say, "Individuals, most notably the great television and radio commentators, make a profession of knowing and saying with elegance and unction what the audience will find most acceptable." He could certainly be writing about some congregations when he describes audiences who display rapt attention but really do not bother to listen because they know what is being said basically confirms them in their own prejudices. They are satisfied simply "to placate the gods by participating in the ritual." Galbraith adds this comment: "No society seems ever to have succumbed to boredom. Man has displayed an obvious capacity for surviving the pompous reiteration of the commonplace."

It might be pertinent to ask whether the pulpit can survive indefinitely the pompous reiteration of the commonplace. Can a pulpit, which is loyal to its prophetic tradition, be satisfied simply to dispense the "conventional wisdom"? Can it proclaim a Gospel of grace but not of judgment? If so, the pulpit has less integrity and less justification for its existence than have other media in culture. Rolf Hochhuth's play, *The Representative* (The Deputy), which exposed the alleged inaction of the Papacy toward the suffering of Jews in Nazi Germany, understandably disturbed and incensed audiences on both sides of the Atlantic. Hochhuth explains his intention in the preface. He says, "The theatre nowadays cannot afford to console itself with being a home for escapism or art-for-art's sake; if it is to survive at all it must fulfil its function as a platform of prophecy, a place in which to judge, to proclaim, to confess and to shock."[8] Neither can the Church now-adays afford to console itself with being a home for escapism or religion-for-religion's sake. If the pulpit is to survive at all it also must fulfil its functions as a platform of prophecy, a place in which to judge, to proclaim, to confess and to shock. Either that, or it is no wonder that young people these days are flocking in greater numbers to the theatres than they are to the churches.

One of the most fascinating paintings of Rembrandt portrays a Hebrew prophet seated on a mountainside and looking down with infinite sorrow on the city beneath him. The great Dutch master has captured in a few strokes of his brush all the loneliness and agony of the prophetic vocation. How welcome the bearer of good news who cheers his contemporaries with a word of comfort and hope! How unwelcome the spokesman for God who confronts men and women with their waywardness, forces them to face their sins, summons them to repentance and threatens them with divine punishment if they fail! The Gospel of God's judgment is never popular but it may be the Gospel that God gives the preacher to proclaim. It is a hopeful Gospel because even as judgment it is still grace, and we can still pray, "Forgive us our sins".

RESURRECTION

Begin with the Resurrection

Paul on Mars Hill spoke to his congregation an authentic word about Resurrection. Declaring that God "has fixed a day on which he will judge the world in righteousness by a man whom he has appointed", he added, "and of this he has given assurance to all men by raising him from the dead". At that point Paul's sermon ended abruptly. We doubt if he intended to end there. Given a chance he would probably have gone on to explain what the Resurrection is all about, but the Athenians didn't give him a chance. "Now when they heard [i.e. the moment they heard] of the resurrection of the dead, some mocked ..."

That's not surprising, because Paul had hit them with something pretty hard to believe. As a Christian missionary he had presumably come to tell them the story of Jesus, yet almost the first thing he said about Jesus was that God raised him from the dead. We should expect Paul to get around to the Resurrection eventually, because that was the climax of Jesus's career, but why start the story with its climax? Why not start further back, telling the Athenians who Jesus was, where he was born and brought up, how he went about teaching people, helping them and healing their sick, how the religious leaders opposed him and put him to death on a cross? Why not prepare their minds and bring them gradually to the breathtaking event of Easter Day? Why must the preacher *begin* with the Resurrection?

Imagine a doctor who discovers a cure for a fatal disease. Overnight he becomes a celebrity. His name makes the newspaper headlines. He is interviewed on television. Publishers want to bring out his biography, because people are interested now in the story of his life. Every detail about him becomes important – his parents, his childhood, his success at medical school, his period as a general practitioner, the long arduous years spent in research, the sacrifice to himself and family. That doctor has won a victory in the battle against death, a victory that gives meaning to all that he is and has ever done. Without it he would be unknown except to the immediate generation of his family, friends, patients and colleagues; and when they pass from the earthly scene, he would be completely forgotten. His victory makes him immortal. Therefore it will always be the important fact about him, the starting-point of his life-story; and from that starting-point people will look back and find significance in the details of his life.

Does that help to explain why Paul in Athens began the story of Jesus with the account of his victory over death? Though Paul had never met the earthly Jesus, he was undoubtedly familiar with the facts of Jesus' birth, life, ministry, teaching and death. Yet those facts were not of first importance to him. The supreme fact about Jesus to which *all* the early apostles bore witness and which they tried to interpret was that God raised him from the dead. In the New Testament the Resurrection is not an epilogue to the story of Jesus; it is the starting-point, the pre-supposition and the effective framework of that story.

The Christian preacher who proclaims a biblical Gospel will begin with the Resurrection. He will treat the Resurrection not as a special piece of music to be played on Easter Sunday but as the great orchestral theme of the Church's worship throughout the Christian year. He will present the Resurrection not as an optional subject to be taken by those who have a mind for it but as a requisite to every man's understanding of the whole Gospel. He will predicate his entire pulpit ministry on the Resurrection and will be very clear in his own mind that every proclamation and every application of the Gospel derives its authority from God's mighty act in raising Jesus from the dead.

The Incarnation

Unless Jesus rose from the dead, how can the preacher proclaim that he was the Son of God? That may not matter to some people in the pews. They are not committed to the Incarnation but are satisfied to accept Jesus as "the man for others" who might have said concerning himself, "God so loved the world that he sent a certain Jew to tell people that there is something to be said for loving one's neighbour." In that case the preacher will need to remind them of certain facts: (1) You do not build churches or create theologies in memory of "a man for others". (2) You do not crucify "a man for others". The religious leaders crucified Jesus because he said "Yes" when Caiaphas demanded, "I adjure you by the living God, tell us if you are the Christ, the Son of God" (Matt. 26:63). (3) You do not follow a dead "man for others". The disciples followed Jesus because they believed that he was "the Christ, the Son of the Living God". (Matt. 16:16) That faith died on Calvary and would have rotted in Joseph's tomb if all that there was of Jesus had rotted in Joseph's tomb. (4) To the men who wrote the New Testament the Resurrection did more than *prove* Jesus to be the son of God; it *made* him the Son of God with power. Peter proclaimed that truth on the day of Pentecost: "Let all the house of Israel therefore know assuredly that God has made him both Lord and Christ, this Jesus whom you crucified" (Acts 2.36). That is why the preacher has to begin with the Resurrection.

Christian Ethics

What validates the teachings of Jesus unless they are the teachings of one whom God raised from the dead? They do not validate themselves. Any man in his right mind who tries to live by the Sermon on the Mount, with its stringent demands for meekness, mercy and magnanimity, will not only have trouble surviving in the jungle of human relations; he might be crucified as Jesus was crucified. Undoubtedly the world would be a happier and more peaceful place if management and labour, Negroes and whites, Arabs and Jews, communists and non-communists, haves and have-nots settled their differences by asking, "What do the teachings of Jesus demand in our situation?" Where would it get them, however, if they laid aside their weapons of coercion and came to the conference table armed with the single weapon of love? We know where it got Jesus – on a Cross. So there's no use the preacher pointing people to the way of Jesus unless he can guarantee that it is God's way and that God has vindicated it and shown it to be eternally right and promised that it will ultimately prevail. The New Testament guarantees that God did vindicate the way of Jesus by raising him from the dead. That's why the preacher has to begin with the Resurrection.

The Atonement
Does not the Resurrection establish the atoning death of Jesus on the Cross? People who are satisfied to believe that it was simply a form of martyrdom, comparable to the shooting down of Martin Luther King in Memphis, need to be reminded that a martyr's death would never have been enough to make the Cross the powerful symbol of Christianity. It would not explain why that instrument of execution has been jealously guarded and retained, given a place of honour in our churches, memorialised in every Sacrament and worn with humility and pride as a piece of costume jewellery. It would not explain why the Cross is the basis of Christian theology and the subject of books written by the greatest thinkers of the centuries. It would not explain why countless men and women, indifferent or even hostile to the dogmas and institutions of religion, have been attracted, changed and redeemed by those two beams of wood set against the background of a blackening sky. At the heart of the Gospel is the conviction that God was on Golgotha doing something supernatural and conclusive about our sins, the conviction that the Cross is the

supreme place of encounter between the love of God and the sin of man, the one place on earth to which a man can come burdened by sin and like Bunyan's Pilgrim feel the burden fall from his back and tumble into the mouth of a sepulchre where it is seen no more. But what if the body of Jesus is still in that sepulchre? What if the Cross killed and defeated him? Not the love of God but the sin of man would have the last word in life and the world; or God was not on the Cross at all, and Christianity is not a Gospel. That's why the preacher has to begin with the Resurrection.

From Death to Life

What about the more daring faith that pulsates through the New Testament, through Christian theology and in the hearts of Christian people, especially as they grow older – the faith that God's love for us, revealed on the Cross of Christ, is so strong that not even death can separate us from it? That faith is our supreme incentive in the Christian life, the beacon of light in the distance that beckons us on and gives us courage to keep going through the darkness of sorrow, suffering, injustice and frustration. It would be terrible if the light in the distance were an optical illusion, as some people would have us believe. When Mr. Krushchev was Prime Minister of Russia he said in a public address, "Comrades, to put it in a nutshell . . . it is not advisable to be in a hurry for the other world. Nobody ever returned from there to report that one lives better there than here . . ." Strangely enough, on the very day – January 16th, 1963 – when the newspapers reported Mr. Krushchev's address, my daily devotions led me to the fifteenth chapter of First Corinthians where Paul, after cataloguing an impressive list of the appearances of one who did return from the other world, asked his readers, "Now if Christ is preached as raised from the dead, how can some of you say that there is no resurrection of the dead?' Contrast Krushchev with Michael Faraday, the scientist who, when he lay dying, was asked, "What are your speculations?" He replied, "Speculations? I have none. I rest my soul on certainties." Those certainties are the Empty Tomb, the Risen Christ, the Gospel and the Church. On what other basis can a preacher speak with conviction about immortality, even to Greek philosophers? That's why the preacher has to begin with the Resurrection.

There is something almost ironic about the rude reaction of the Greek philosophers to Paul's sermon on Mars Hill. According to the New Testament those first century eggheads "spent their time in nothing except telling or hearing about something new"; and when Paul stood up to address them, they patronisingly asked, "What will this babbler say . . . . What new thing will he tell us?" They mocked when Paul told them that God raised Jesus from the dead. They mocked because they were too intellectually proud to realise that they were, in fact, hearing about something new, the only radically new thing which had happened since the dawn of Creation, an event that remade Creation and started history all over again.

The writers of the New Testament saw the Resurrection of Christ as a mighty act of God that inaugurated a new age upon this earth. Like the explosion of the first atomic bomb it shook the this earth and the heavens and sent its reverberations to the farthest reaches of the universe. It changed everything for every man, woman and child in the world, so that life on this earth could never be the same again. As one scientist wrote, after he had helped to create the bomb, "Man must now go the way of Jesus or perish". But the point is that we *can* go the way of Jesus and *not* perish. That is the new thing that Paul told the philosophers, the new thing that God has done, the new choice that the Resurrection of Christ gives to the human race and to each one of us – the choice of life instead of death. That's why the preacher has to begin with the Resurrection.

CHAPTER NOTES

1 *Religion in Life*, Spring 1969, pp. 92–101.
2 D. R. Davies, *In Search of Myself* (Bles, London, 1961), pp. 68–72.
3 Karl Barth, *Church Dogmatics* (Clark, Edinburgh, 1957), Vol. II, "The Doctrine of God", Part I, p. 3.
4 S.C.M. Press, London, 1967, p. 21 ff.
5 The theme of my book, *God in Man's Experience* (Hodder and Stoughton, London, 1968).
6 Pierre Berton, *The Comfortable Pew* (Hodder and Stoughton, London, 1965).
7 *The Affluent Society*, pp. 17–26.
8 Methuen, London, 1963, p. xi.

CHAPTER FOUR

The Unknown God

"What therefore you worship as unknown, this I proclaim
to you".   *Acts* 17:23

It is not an uncommon experience in life to be closely associated with a person, yet not really know him. You may work for
that person, be a part of the organisation which he owns and
directs, see him from time to time and feel the impact of his life
upon yours, yet you may have a mental image of him which is
totally inadequate because you don't really know him. Maybe
you've got him pegged as a cross between Caligula and Attila the
Hun. You describe your mental image to one of his friends who
laughs and says, "But he isn't like that at all. He's charming and
witty and generous and sensitive. He lives modestly, he likes flow-
ers and music, he loves children, he's kind to his mother-in-law.
It's obvious that you don't know him the way I do."

Have you never wanted to say the same thing about God to the
articulate atheists whose image of him is so patently inadequate?
You ask yourself, "Who is this God that they are trying to knock
out of the sky?" Reading their magazine articles and listening
to their radio broadcasts, you scarcely recognise the Deity against
whom they bear such a grudge. Wherever they formed their mental image of God, whether in Sunday School or in their fresh-
man year at university, it is an image that most intelligent people
ceased to hold a long time ago. If there is agony in atheism,
there is also a vast reservoir of ignorance. We respect honest
doubt but we cannot help feeling that many disbelievers are tilting
at a God whom they don't really know.

Lord Altrincham laid some of the blame on the Churches.
Writing in the *Guardian* a few years ago, he was commenting on

Sir Julian Huxley's book, *The Humanist Frame*, which gave God
the brush-off and asserted that "evolutionary man can no longer
take refuge from his loneliness by creeping for shelter into the
arms of a divinised father-figure whom he has himself created. . ."
Lord Altrincham gave his opinion that "organised religion is largely to blame for the fact that a man as intelligent and altogether
admirable as Sir Julian Huxley should be capable of writing such
nonsense." He believed that the God whom Huxley dismissed
"is the parsonical God – a metaphysical amalgam of Pope John,
Dr. Ramsay, Mr. Ben-Gurion and President Makarios. It is not
the Lord Omnipotent, unimaginable yet indispensable, remote yet
immediate, whose creatures we are, whose inscrutable purposes
we serve". He added, "The Churches present a picture of Deity
. . . which is so trivial and banal that the mystical conscience, if
combined with any critical faculty, is bound to reject it."

The situation is this: Just as unbelievers may be ignorant of
the God whom they deny, so believers may be ignorant of the
God whom they worship. Their religion brings them into touch
with God, but God himself is unknown to them. Paul found that
situation in ancient Athens. As he wandered through the streets
he saw shrines and monuments on every corner, as profuse as the
church buildings in Toronto, and he concluded, as a visitor to
our city might conclude, that the people were very religious.
Tucked away among these many shrines and monuments was a
little altar which bore the interesting inscription, "To an unknown God". Scholars have difficulty identifying it. Some suggest
that it may have been a Jewish altar; others think that it might
have been like the tomb of the unknown soldier – a token recognition of any gods not already named and recognised in the
Greek Pantheon. At any rate, Paul seized on that little shrine and
made it the jumping-off point of his sermon to the Greek philosophers on Mars Hill: "Men of Athens, I perceive that in every
way you are very religious. For as I passed along, and observed
the objects of your worship, I found also an altar with the inscription, 'To an unknown God'. What therefore you worship as unknown, this I proclaim to you". Paul was saying to the Athenians,
"There is, in fact, an unknown God who is greater, grander,
more mysterious and more magnificent than all the little deities

represented by your religion, and I want to tell you some things about him."

I

First, "The God who made the world and everything in it, being Lord of heaven and earth, does not live in shrines made by man, nor is he served by human hands, as though he needed anything, since he himself gives to all men life and breath and everything."

The Greek philosophers would not have to be convinced of the existence of a Creator, nor would most philosophers who hold a more-than-humanistic view of life and the universe. They believed that the world had a First Cause, a Prime Mover, an Intelligent Creator and Designer. They conceded that life itself can be traced to a Source just as a mighty river can be traced to its source, and they might call this Uncreated Source of All Creation by the name "God." It didn't follow, however, that they *knew* God the Creator any more than they knew a famous artist simply by giving him credit for one of his masterpieces. They had not necessarily encountered God in his Creation. God the Creator may have been unknown to them.

Paul, on the other hand, was a Jew whose mind was steeped in the Old Testament, especially the opening verse of the first chapter of Genesis: "In the beginning God created the heavens and the earth . . ." Get one thing clear – the Jews were not nature-worshippers; they were materialists. Unlike the Greeks they drew no false dichotomy between the material and the spiritual. For them the material world was shot through with spiritual meaning; it was their place of encounter with God. "The heavens declare the glory of God; and the firmament showeth his handiwork."[1] Every part of creation spoke to the Jews of their Creator. Sunset and dawn, winter and summer told them that behind this orderly dependable universe is a creative Spirit ever intelligent and supremely loving. The receding waves on the seashore told them that God who sets boundaries for the ocean tides also sets boundaries for the destructive elements that beat on the shore of man's soul. The wild flower in the desert told them that the God who lavishes love on the waste and desolate ground will not forget men and women in their waste and desolate hearts.

Wasn't it exciting on Christmas Eve, 1968, when the Apollo 8 astronauts, on man's first journey around the moon, greeted the human race 250,000 miles away not with a moral message peculiar to the Christian festival of peace and goodwill but with the majestic words of the opening chapter of Genesis, "In the beginning God created the heavens and the earth . . ."? That was obviously the tremendous truth that gripped their minds as they cruised among the stars and saw the vastness of the universe and realised the genius of the human brain that could conceive and carry out such an incredible journey. Creation brought them face to face with God the Creator. And wasn't it exciting how the human race responded to the astronauts' words, re-broadcasting them in many languages over radio networks in the free world and the communist world alike? Of course, Mrs. Madelyn Murray O'Hair was not pleased. She started an agitation to force Congress to pass a law prohibiting the reading of Scriptures from outer space – presumably because she herself has never encountered God the Creater in inner space. She is not alone in her spiritual ignorance. God the Creator is unknown to many people. "What therefore you worship as unknown, this I proclaim to you".

II

The next thing Paul told the Athenians about God is that "he made from one every nation of men to live on all the face of the earth, having determined allotted periods and the boundaries of their habitation . . ."

It was surely a daring claim to make – that God has anything to do with the genetics of the human race, the life-span of civilisations and the arrangement of national boundaries. Yet the Bible makes that claim all the way through. The Bible insists that, having created the world, God did not then withdraw to a distant heaven and leave his Creation to run itself. Having peopled the earth with a race of men who have human needs and problems, God accepts responsibility for them, meets their needs and helps them to solve their problems. Having set history in motion, God presides over history, involves himself in history and directs history according to his wise and loving purpose. God is not only the Creator. He is Sovereign.

The men who wrote the Bible proclaimed God's sovereignty not as a theological doctrine but as a fact which they had experienced. They had certainly experienced it in their life as a nation. Looking back over the events of their history, they saw it as a drama directed by God. Even the tragic scenes in the drama, even the sinister characters who appeared on the stage seemed to have their proper place in the divine plan. Thus Isaiah could describe the pagan King of Assyria as "the rod of [God's] anger", a dead, unconscious instrument that God was using to promote his own purposes.[2] God's people recognised his sovereignty over their personal lives. Joseph in Egypt could say to his jealous brothers who had sold him into slavery, "And now do not be distressed, or angry with yourselves, because you sold me here; for God sent me before you to preserve life."[3]

There was a time when life had become so empty and hopeless for William Cowper, the English poet, that he decided to end it all by committing suicide. Hailing a horse-drawn cab, he told the driver to take him to one of the bridges over the River Thames. He was not the first or last man in London who has looked at the Thames and felt like jumping into it. It was a foggy night, however, and the fog was so dense that the cab driver couldn't find the Thames but kept going around the streets in circles. After an hour of this, Cowper ordered him to stop, thrust open the door of the cab and stepped out. He expected to see the river but discovered instead that he was right back at his own doorstep. Smitten by the coincidence, he rushed to his room, took a quill and paper and wrote the lines which have kindled faith in countless hearts:

"God moves in a mysterious way
His wonders to perform . . ."

But the God who "moves in a mysterious way", or moves at all, is unknown to many people, even religious people. They swallow the big lie that God is dead, because God has never been alive for them. They have never encountered a living God, never consciously experienced his providence, never recognised his sovereignty over their lives. They cannot look back and recall one specific instance where a more-than-human factor intervened in their affairs. They cannot look out on the affairs of the world and discern what the poet called "a power not our own that works for righteousness". So it's no wonder that religion bores them after a while, and the Church seems like a museum, and worship leaves them cold, and prayer becomes an exercise in futility. They believe in God but not a sovereign God who rules and governs and controls and acts. That God is unknown to them. "What therefore you worship as unknown, this I proclaim to you."

III

Paul says something else about God: "We ought not to think that the Deity is like gold, or silver, or stone, a representation by the art and imagination of man."

As a devout Jew Paul would have an ingrained prejudice against anything that smacked of idolatry. Did not the commandment say, "You shall not make yourself a graven image"?[4] The Jews objected to material symbols of God not only because they stole the glory of God but because they represented the fundamental fallacy, from which the Jews themselves were not free, that God can be localised and contained. Paul was telling the Athenians that you cannot do that with God, you cannot cut him down to your size, you cannot reduce him to anything human.

During the war a navy chaplain preached a power-packed sermon on the Ten Commandments. One sailor left the service feeling guilty for having done evil in the sight of the Lord all up and down the line. He brightened, however, and said to himself, "Well, at least I've never worshipped a graven image." He was probably wrong. What is a graven image in modern terms? Anything that man creates and makes a more certain basis of faith than God himself. Gold and silver and stone are not the only human idolatries. Paul's sermon updated might go like this: "We ought not to think that the Deity is like books or buildings or ideas or emotions, representations by the thought and imagination of man". In other words, don't get the idea that the Creator and Sovereign of the universe can be bound by the Bible or boxed up in the Church or contained in theology or reduced to a human emotion like love. Grab that kind of God and you have got not God but only an idol of your own devising.

Why has the word "Supernatural" suddenly become a dirty word even in the vocabulary of religious people? Why do men try to cut God down to their own size and make him over again in their own image? Do they not know the God of the Bible, "the high and lofty One who inhabits eternity, whose name is Holy"?[5] That God is precisely super-nature, above and beyond nature; he is God and not man. We don't create him; he creates us. We don't judge him; he judges us. There is a story about an audience who filled a theatre to watch a play. When the curtain went up, the first audience found themselves gazing at another crowd on the stage watching them. That went on for three acts. At length, the first audience became disturbed because they had come to the theatre to watch, not to be watched. Isn't that how we stand in relation to God?

"Why God Has Allowed Us Into Space"[6] is the title of a magazine interview with Wernher von Braum, the scientific genius behind America's space programme. It was he who developed the mighty engines which provided the nine million pounds of thrust that sent Apollo 9 on its way to a moon landing. Dr. von Braun grew up in the Church but he says that the importance and the need of religion became apparent to him only when he began to explore the vast mysteries of the universe and to realise the immense power at man's disposal. He finds it as difficult to understand scientists who do not acknowledge the presence of a superior rationality behind the universe as it is to understand theologians who do not acknowledge the advances of science. He says, "We must learn to consider God as Creator of the universe and Master of everything. We need a greater Lord than we have had in the past." Dr. von Braun believes that God intends man to explore the other planets just as he intended him to explore this planet; otherwise he would not have given man the curiosity, the intelligence and the tools for space travel. It is obvious that this great scientist does not reduce the Supernatural God to the sum total of everything good or loving in man's nature. He says, "Astronomy and space explorations are teaching us that the good Lord is a much greater Lord and Master of a greater Kingdom."

Yet that God is still unknown to many people. "What therefore you worship as unknown, this I proclaim to you."

IV

The last thing Paul says about God is that "he is not far from each one of us", and he adds the quotation, "In him we live and move and have our being."

"Where do we find God?" is the question brought into focus by John A. T. Robinson's book, *Honest to God*. He reminds us that we used to look for God "up there", but modern astronomy makes that search ridiculous. Then we looked for God "out there", but space travel knocked him out of that sky. Instead, we are supposed to look for God "in here" and think of him not as a Being separate and distinct from the world which he has created but as Being Itself, the Ground and Depth of All Being. So the debate continues but with curious disregard of the Bible which sees things the other way round. The Bible does not locate God somewhere in the stars; it locates the stars in him. It does not look for God in the universe, because God is bigger than the universe; he contains the universe. God is not in us; we are in God. He is "our dwelling place in all generations".[7] "In him we live and move and have our being."

So, of course, God "is not far from each one of us". Restated positively, he is close to each one of us, "nearer than breathing, closer than hands and feet". God is the very atmosphere in which we live, the oxygen we breathe, the sunlight that brightens the world and gives warmth to the earth. It is not only true that we can reach out and touch God; it is even more true that we can never escape him. "Whither shall I go from thy spirit? or whither shall I flee from thy presence?"[8] We can know this God, we can consciously commune with him. "Were I a preacher," wrote Brother Lawrence, "I should above all other things preach the practice of the presence of God", and he did preach that message by his own devout life in the noise and clutter of the monastery kitchen where he said, "I possess God in as great tranquillity as if I were on my knees at the Blessed Sacrament."

There was a time when men were very sure that "God is not far from each of us". They saw him incarnated in a human personality, a man who was bone of their bone and flesh of their flesh and who stood beside them and shared their every human experience. When we talk about the Incarnation let's be clear what it means. We do not claim that God vacated his throne in outer space and came like a visitor from another planet and for a time walked about the earth disguised as a man. We do claim that the Creator, Sovereign, Transcendent God, in whom we live and move and have our being, filled a human life with his presence and thereby showed us once and for all what he is like. Man looked into the compassionate eyes of Jesus, they felt the touch of his healing hand on their bodies and souls, they saw the sheer goodness and purity of his character, they heard the words of love and wisdom that came from his lips and they said simply, "God must be like Jesus. He is the visible image of the invisible God."

Try an experiment with yourself. Say the word "God" and see what comes into your mind. Nothing, perhaps, but a vague, oblong blur. When Paul spoke the name of God, the Athenian philosophers would think only of abstract ideas. Paul would think of a Person, a man who lived and died and rose from the dead, whose living presence arrested him on the Damascus Road and changed the whole course of his career. Paul believed that Jesus was the only God whom any man could know as a constant companion and friend on life's journey. Yet many people do not know him. They continue, as Paul says, to "seek God, in the hope that they might feel after him and find him". They do not know the God who has sought and found us in Jesus. That God is still unknown to them. "What therefore you worship as unknown, this I proclaim to you."

CHAPTER NOTES

1   Psalm 19:1.
2   Isaiah 10:5.
3   Genesis 45:5 R.S.V.
4   Exodus 20:4 R.S.V.
5   Isaiah 57:15 R.S.V.
6   Adon Taft in *Christian Life*, July, 1969.
7   Psalm 90:1 R.S.V.
8   Psalm 139:7 R.S.V.

F

CHAPTER FIVE

As the Bible Sees You

There is a striking line in Eugene O'Neill's fantastic play, *The Great God Brown*. When the central figure, Brown, lies dead on the street, a policeman bends over his body and asks, "Well, what's his name?" Someone replies, "Man." Then the policeman, with notebook and pencil, demands, "How do you spell it?"

Isn't that one of the basic questions of our time and all time – How do you spell the word "man"? Large areas of society spell it "s-l-a-v-e". You may be surprised to know that slavery is still practised in certain areas of the world, even countries where it has been officially abolished. It is estimated that in the Middle East and Africa today more than five million persons have been sold and bought like machinery or cattle. Some governments practise a form of slavery. In an outspoken sermon at the St. Augustine Church in Warsaw the Roman Catholic Primate of Poland asked, "How long do we have to work until a citizen in his own country really becomes a citizen, not a slave...?"[1] Even in the "free" world there are some employers who treat their employees, some husbands who treat their wives, some children who treat their parents, like slaves.

At the opposite extreme are those who spell man's name "m-a-s-t-e-r". That daring insight emerges from the eighth Psalm written in a pre-scientific age by a Hebrew poet who stood under the Judean night sky and prayed to God, "When I consider thy heavens, the work of thy fingers, the moon and stars which thou hast ordained; What is man that thou art mindful of him...?" That God should do for man what he does not do for all the planets and solar systems staggered the Psalmist, and he concluded that God must have created man for a high and worthy purpose. That purpose, he declared in a mighty outburst of praise, is mastery. Man is made for mastery over all animate and inanimate creation. "Thou madest him to have dominion over the works of the hands; thou hast put all things under his feet . . ."

How do you spell the word "man"? It is a basic question, and the answer is usually as plain as a pikestaff. Once, when he was in command of a frigate in the Mediterranean, Lord Nelson heard the cry, "Man overboard!"; and though he knew that the enemy was close behind, he ordered the ship stopped and a small boat sent out to search for the missing sailor. That's how Nelson spelled the word "man". At the age of thirty Albert Schweitzer gave up brilliant careers in music, philosophy and theology, studied medicine and went to spend the rest of his life healing sick people in French Equatorial Africa. That's how he spelled the word "man". At the height of the Korean War a newspaper cartoon showed someone telling Mao-Tsetung about the rising rate of Korean casualties. The Chinese leader is shrugging his shoulders and retorting, "There are plenty of Koreans." That is how he spelled the word "man". Everything we decide and say and do in relation to ourselves and to other people is determined basically by our spelling of the word "man". The neurotic who cuts his wrist, the hippie who lives on heroin, the woman who sells her body, the executive who destroys his competitors, the teacher who cares deeply for her pupils are all motivated by their particular view of the nature and destiny of man.

How does the Bible spell the word "man"? We could find our answer in the first chapter of Genesis or the eighth Psalm or the teachings of Jesus but we shall look for it in a less likely place – the sermon that Paul preached to the Greek philosophers on Mars Hill in Athens. To be sure, it was mainly a sermon about God, but that very fact makes it also a sermon about man. From every truth that the apostle told the Athenians about God we can infer certain truths about man.

I

By affirming that God is Creator, Paul implies that man is

a creature. That is one Bible spelling of man's name. So states the Bible in its very first chapter: "God created man in his own image . . . male and female he created them."[2] That is not a scientific statement; it has nothing to do with man's descent from the apes. John Doe, the great grandson of Ebenezer Doe, may trace his ancestry a long way back, but to say that he is a creature is to make a theological statement. It means simply that neither he nor his great grandfather created themselves. Both were created by God who, as Paul says, "gives to all men life and breath and everything".

That is exactly the truth about himself that man tends to forget or chooses to ignore. Even his first ancestors overlooked it when a snake appeared in the garden and told them how they could make themselves equal to God.[3] Now especially, when man's creative powers have given him such unprecedented mastery over the rest of God's creation, he quickly forgets that he himself is one of God's creatures. Man has become so intoxicated with his own creative genius that he fancies himself as God's partner and after a while begins to behave as though God had retired and given him control of the business.

We must not put the blame on Dietrich Bonhoeffer whose classic phrase about man's "coming of age" has been ripped out of context and bandied about by people who have not done their homework. Writing from his prison cell in Nazi Germany, Bonhoeffer did not foresee a world without God. He did foresee man coming of age as every child comes of age. When that happens, the child's father gives him more and more responsibility for his own life but he doesn't cease to be a father. Instead, the relationship between father and son grows and develops; it becomes deeper, richer, more precious and more demanding than it was in the boy's childhood. That's a far cry from the modern titanism that rebels against God, like a crowd of juveniles rebelling against their college president, and kicks him out of his office as though he were a senile old man. The prophet Isaiah came closer to the mood of our time when he thundered, "Woe to him who strives with his Maker, an earthen vessel with the potter! Does the clay say to him who fashions it, 'What are you making'? or 'Your work has no handles'?"[4]

Among the letters to the newspaper when Bertrand Russell
died was a gloating one that held up the British mathematician
as proof that a man can live a good, long and useful life without
the superstitions of religion. Such letters deserve no reply, but it
might be pointed out to the writer that there have been men of
equal stature with Lord Russell who humbly acknowledged themselves as creatures of God. When Emerson Hall was being built
at Harvard University, the faculty decided that upon the frieze
there should be a carved quotation from Protagoras: "Man is
the measure of all things." President Elliot decided differently.
The faculty dispersed for the summer holidays and when they returned they found the frieze complete and inscribed with the
words of the eighth Psalm: "What is man that thou art mindful of him?"

II

When Paul goes on to describe God's concern for his human
creatures, we infer that man is very dear to God, he has a special
place in the scheme of things, he differs from the rest of God's
creation, he is *a child of God.* That is another truth about himself that man tends to forget. In fact, our culture displays a curious ambivalence, seen, for example, in the surprising musical
revue, *Hair,* which sets to music the words of Shakespeare, "What
a piece of work (murk) is man! ... In apprehension how like an
angel and in comprehension how like God!", yet in its total
message stresses man's kinship with the apes. What a low view
of man emerges from much modern literature! Some novelists
give the impression that they have never met a good man or a
nice woman or seen the inside of a Christian home. They have the
jungle mentality which sees man as a creature of the jungle and
ridicules his efforts to be anything different.

We thank God for literature that provides a refreshing contrast.
In a hospital one day I found a patient reading A. S. M. Hutchinson's novel, *If Winter Comes.* He told me that he was reading it
for the third time. He said that he kept coming back to it, because
it is the kind of literature that restores his faith in human nature.
We can appreciate what he meant. Through the story runs a
streak of lust and meanness and hypocrisy, yet in the hero, Mark

Sabre, and his few loyal friends Hutchinson leaves you with the impression that there is something basically decent and noble in man, something that bears the image of the Divine.

In the truth that we are children of God we find our proper place in the affections of God and our significance as human beings. Halford Luccock, who was a good Methodist, reminds us that Susanna Wesley had nineteen children, a large family even in those days and even for so competent a mother. He humorously suggests that she got their clothes mixed on occasion but he asks more seriously, "Do you imagine she ever got *them* mixed? Did Samuel sort of fade into John, and was Charles a misty blending of both? Would she have cared little if one had slipped out of her life, finding ready comfort in the fact that she had eighteen left? If you have any doubt about it read her letters to her children. Each one had his own individual place that none of the others, not all eighteen together, could fill."[5] To a loving parent each child is unique and irreplaceable; and if that is true of human parents, how infinitely more true, as Jesus said, of the Father God!

During World War Two Hitler sent his bully boys to Bethel Hospital to inform its director that the state could no longer afford to maintain hundreds of useless epileptics and that orders had been issued to have them destroyed. The director blocked their path with a single weapon. That weapon was the simple affirmation that these were men and women made in the image of God and that to destroy them would be to commit an unpardonable sin against God. What other argument could he have used? What other argument can *we* use against power politics that allows innocent babies to die of hunger? What other argument against obsolescent laws that penalise a man for the colour of his skin? What other argument against a dehumanising collectivism which teaches that society is everything and the individual nothing? What other argument against a civilisation so mechanised, computerised and standardised that it pulverises personality and reduces the human soul from one to zero?

III

Referring to their idolatries, Paul told the Athenians, "The times of ignorance God overlooked, but now he commands all men everywhere to repent . . ." Presumably it implies that man needs to repent. He is a child of God but a disobedient child, *a sinner*. That's another Bible spelling of man's name.

Plenty of people don't like the word. They refuse to be designated sinners, because sin suggests guilt, and guilt for past errors is not a characteristic of the "now generation", even those who go to Church. An elderly retired minister said recently that, whereas in any congregation sixty years ago you could count on a general sense of guilt, now the only thing you can count on is a general sense of doubt. So there's no use trying to convert people by convincing them, as Paul writes elsewhere, that we "all have sinned and fall short of the glory of God".[6] Possibly not, but the Bible has more than one definition of sin. See how the New English Bible translates Paul's statement: "For all alike have sinned, and are deprived of the divine splendour." We are to think of sin not as something we have *done* but as something we have *missed*. What have we missed? The splendour of manhood that God revealed in the man Jesus.

In the Louvre Gallery in Paris you will be shown a famous piece of sculpture called "The Gladiator". It is a life-sized statue of a Greek athlete poised in the act of throwing the discus. The artist, whose name can be faintly deciphered in the marble, took perfection as his model – a human figure, beautiful to behold, ideally proportioned and perfect in symmetry. So life-like are the straining sinews, the protruding veins and iron muscles that doctors sometimes use this statue as a model for their lectures in anatomy. Here indeed is the model of physical manhood, the human physique at its best, the likeness in chiselled marble of that perfect manliness which is the dream of every red-blooded, growing boy.

On the morning that my wife and I visited the Louvre we noticed something rather pathetic – a group of shabbily dressed French boys, accompanied by a teacher, obviously on an educational tour. Whenever they stood before a work of art, the teacher took each lad, guided his fingers over it and carefully described its appearance. One guessed immediately that the boys were blind. Deprived of sight, they must appreciate the treasures of the

Louvre through touch and hearing. The teacher took one small fellow in his arms and lifted him up so that he could touch "The Gladiator". The contrast brought tears to my eyes. Here was a thin, spindly-legged little child reaching up to embrace this specimen in marble of perfect physical manhood.

It seemed like a parable. Christ is the Gladiator, the model not only of physical manhood but of full-orbed human personality. In him personality found its highest expression. He made of our manhood the most splendid thing ever to appear on this earth. Christ is the Representative Man, the Man par excellence, the true splendour of manhood as God created it and as God intended it to be; and by contrast we know ourselves to be as emaciated and deprived as the little blind boy in the Louvre. That's what the Bible means by the Fall of Man which it sees not only as an event in the past but as a spiritual condition which is constantly present. We are not aware of it until we come into the spiritual Louvre and look at ourselves before the spiritual Gladiator. Then we know that we "have sinned and fall short of the Glory of God". We know that we "are deprived of the divine splendour".

IV

Yet we cannot look at Jesus for very long without looking at his Cross. Paul on Mars Hill did not mention the Cross, though it was never far from his mind, and he certainly suggested it by his allusion to divine judgment. To Paul and to all the writers of the New Testament the final truth about man is not that he is a creature, a child of God, a disobedient child, but that he is *a child for whom Christ died.*

That puts a very high value on man; it provides the ultimate criterion for establishing his worth as a human being. We have our own criteria by which to measure human worth, and their importance varies in different social settings. Someone has said that in Washington the first question asked about a man is, "Where does he come from?"; in New York, "How much money has he made?"; in Chicago, "What has he done?"; and in Boston, "What is his family background?" Other societies determine a man's value by the length of his nose, the colour of his skin, the accent of his speech or the name of his religion. Such questions have no relevance in the Bible where the final truth about any person, regardless of his colour, creed or credit-rating, is the truth that he is a man for whom Christ died.

What do we mean by calling ourselves "men for whom Christ died"? We could easily settle for a half-truth and explain the Cross exclusively in terms of its moral influence, comparing Christ's death to the vicarious death of a parent for his child or the supreme sacrifice of soldiers in war. No man with a moral sense can fail to be profoundly stirred by the awareness that someone has believed in him and loved him enough to die for him. That accounts partially for the impact of the Cross, simply because it *is* the Cross of Christ and because it brought to fulfilment his life of incredible faith and love. Whoever stands on Calvary's Hill and looks into the face of the Crucified must echo the words of Charles Wesley:

> "And can it be that I should gain
>   An interest in the Saviour's blood?
> Died He for me, who caused His pain;
>   For me, who Him to death pursued?
> Amazing love! how can it be
>   That Thou, my God, shouldst die for me?"

Yet that does not really explain how the Cross establishes the worth of each human being regardless of whether he consciously stands before it. Consider this parallel. It is said that at the funeral procession of Abraham Lincoln a Negro mother lifted her child above the heads of the crowd and said, "Take a good look at that man. He died to set you free." That was true. What Lincoln had done during his presidency would affect that child and his children and his children's children. By abolishing slavery Lincoln had radically and decisively changed the situation of all the future generations of Negroes in America. In the same light the Bible sees the Cross of Christ. God was on Golgotha. It was God's mighty act whereby he once and for all broke the enslaving power of evil that estranged us from him, so that now we are free to go back to God and live as the obedient children of his

89

love. The Cross does more than lay a moral obligation on us. It changes our status as human beings. It makes us men for whom Christ died.

Dickens in his *Tale of Two Cities* tells of a prisoner in the Bastille who lived in a cell and cobbled shoes for many years and who became so enamoured of the narrow walls, the darkness and the task's monotony that, when liberated, he built a cell at the centre of his English home; and on days when the sun was shining and the birds were singing, the tap of his cobbler's hammer in the dark could still be heard. That could be another parable. We ask ourselves, how does the Bible see us? It sees us exactly as we choose to be; for the choice is ours – either to exist as prisoners in moral darkness or to open the door which Christ has unlocked and go out to the free life of the sons of God.

CHAPTER NOTES

1   January 31, 1965.
2   Genesis 1:27 R.S.V.
3   Genesis 3:5.
4   Isaiah 45:9 R.S.V.
5   Halford Luccock, *Marching off the Map* (Harper, New York, 1952), p. 84.
6   Romans 3:23 R.S.V.

CHAPTER SIX

The Appointed Judge

'... he has fixed a day on which he will judge the world in righteousness by a man whom he has appointed. . ."

Acts 17:31

The President of the United States must have been acutely embarrassed. In 1969 he appointed a well-known Southern lawyer to the Supreme Court, but Congress refused to ratify the appointment on the grounds that the appointee had a known record of race prejudice and would therefore not judge all men impartially. If those who blackballed the prospective judge had their facts straight, we can only commend their caution. No man should be more carefully chosen than a judge or a magistrate. He should be appointed, not elected, and appointed not for his service to a political party but for his expertise in the law and his wisdom in dispensing justice.[1] A judge carries an almost Godlike responsibility in that he may exercise the power of life and death over those who stand before him accused of crimes. Of any man appointed to the Bench we have a right to ask, "What is he like? Is he a humane kind of man? Will he be fair in his judgments? Will he show mercy?"

To most of us those are academic questions because, unless we plan to ignore the occasional parking fine, we are not likely to find ourselves in a courtroom at the mercy of a judge. That is one of the blessed features of life in the "free" world that those who romanticise other social systems are inclined to forget. Suppose, however, we could be absolutely certain that we shall eventually stand before a Bench where our fate will be decided not for a few years but for all eternity? *Then* we might ask questions about the character of the Judge. Suppose we knew that the whole world of men and nations is destined to be judged ultimately? Then we should want to know what sort of person the Judge will be.

When the Apostle Paul preached to the Greek Philosophers on Mars Hill in ancient Athens he referred to their idolatries as belonging to an age of ignorance which God in his mercy over-looked. Paul went on to point out that the age of ignorance is over. With the coming of Christ the age of enlightenment has begun. "But now," said Paul, "he commands all men everywhere to repent, because he has fixed a day on which he will judge the world in righteousness by a man whom he has appointed . . ." If Paul spoke the truth, we *are* going to be judged – all of us. God has fixed the day of judgment and he has appointed the Judge. That Judge is Jesus Christ.

I

Right away a host of difficulties come tumbling into our minds. We have difficulty visualising Jesus as judge; it is not the picture of him that emerges from the Gospels. Jesus attracts us because, unlike the scribes and Pharisees, he did not judge people. He accepted even the worst of them, stood by them, comforted them, healed them and redeemed them. The classic example is the woman caught in the act of adultery whom the religious leaders would have stoned to death had not Jesus restrained them and said to her, "Neither do I condemn thee: go, and sin no more."[2] Surely that means everything to our understanding of God. Some religions and some forms of Christianity cling to the image of God as Judge on a Bench, but if God is like Jesus he regards us ultimately not with judgment but with love.

Yet is not judgment one of the qualities of love? When a boy gets into serious trouble he will do everything possible to prevent his parents from finding out. He may not care what other people think about him, but the last people whom he wants to face are his mother and father. Why? Because he loves them and doesn't want to hurt them and because he knows that their love for him will be a judgment that pierces the heart and goes far deeper than the cutting censure of society.

Anyone who has trouble visualising Jesus as judge needs to read the New Testament more carefully. Because he loved people

Jesus inevitably judged them. He judged them by what he said – calling the Pharisees "whitewashed tombs, which outwardly appear beautiful, but within are full of dead men's bones and all uncleanness".[3] Jesus judged people by what he did – turning over the tables of the moneychangers in the temple and accusing them of making God's house of prayer "a den of robbers".[4] He judged people by the way he looked at them – sending the cowardly disciple, who had denied him in the courtyard of Caiaphas, out into the darkness to weep bitterly.[5] He judged people by what he was. Again it was Peter who, recognising the moral chasm between himself and Jesus, cried out, "Depart from me, for I am a sinful man, O Lord."[6]

Men crucified Jesus because he judged them. His very presence made them so uncomfortable that they had only two alternatives – either to be like him or to get rid of him, and they chose to get rid of him. In a motion picture scene which shows a jailbreak the escaping prisoners, armed with machine-guns, make the searchlight their first target. They must smash that glaring light if they hope to be free to get away in the darkness. Think of that figure in relation to Jesus's claim, "I am the light of the world."[7] A searchlight reveals, exposes, judges. Only a man with nothing to hide can stand its blinding glare. Other men have no alternative but to smash it. That's what men tried to do with Jesus, the Light of the World – smash him by nailing him to a Cross.

II

But, "The light shines in the darkness, and the darkness has not overcome it."[8] The Cross was itself God's giant searchlight, God's supreme act of judgment; and that partially answers another question that puzzles us when we grapple with Paul's sermon to the Greek philosophers. Jesus the appointed Judge – we may be willing to go along with that. We don't respond so readily to the idea of God's having "fixed a day on which he will judge the world in righteousness". To begin with, our imagination boggles at the thought of all the people who ever lived crowding into a cosmic courtroom for a last great assize. In fact, we are just about ready to jettison Judgment Day theology until we realise that Paul could be talking about a day not in the future but in the past. There was a day when God judged the world in righteousness by a man whom he appointed. That day was Good Friday.

Of course, to someone who opens the New Testament and reads the story of Good Friday for the first time it may seem that things were the other way around and that Jesus himself was the one being judged. But things are not always the way they seem. When Dietrich Bonhoeffer was a professor at the University of Berlin, the faculty invited Karl Barth to appear before them and defend his theological position. It was upsetting to the young Bonhoeffer who wrote in one of his letters, "It was not a pretty picture... Barth like a prisoner at the bar, sitting on a little chair, had to give an account of himself to these great men of the Church. Then, on his request that the questions might begin, there followed a long uncomfortable silence, because no one wanted to be the first to make a fool of himself..."[9] Bonhoeffer need not have been upset, because obviously Barth was not on trial before his inquisitors; they were on trial before him.

It has become commonplace to say that such was the situation on Good Friday. Everybody knows who was really on trial – not Jesus but his accusers and his executioners. He stood in the prisoner's dock, they sat on the bench; but they weren't judging Jesus, he was judging them. They stand forever condemned by the man whom God has appointed to judge the world in righteousness. If they could all be brought to trial, Nuremberg style, in some eternal courtroom and charged with the corporate crime of Calvary, the charge would go like this: "... did wilfully premeditate and on the morning of Friday... in the year of our Lord 29 carry out and execute the murder of one Jesus of Nazareth... Do you plead guilty or not guilty?" All would have to plead guilty.

Not those men alone, however, but all whom they represent stand judged before the Cross. There are two human factors in the Cross of Christ: a morally perfect life and a concentration of evil that violently assaulted that life and tried to destroy it. Like a giant searchlight the Cross exposed every wickedness of which the human heart is capable. It exposed the treachery that sells its soul for silver. It exposed the cowardice that denies friendship to save its own skin. It exposed the intrigue that sacrifices human life for the sake of vested interests. It exposed the hypocrisy that destroys the innocent to protect its own position. It exposed the fickleness that prefers a common criminal to the best of men. It exposed the violence sanctioned by law that turns men into beasts. It exposed the dumb acquiescence that connives at crime simply by staring at it. These are not factors that remain locked in history; they are real factors in business, politics, industry, diplomacy and all areas of man's life today; you can read about them on the front page of any newspaper. They stand forever judged by the Cross of Christ.

III

Try to imagine a company of athletes in training for the Olympics. They are preparing themselves for the day when a super-athlete will come to the training camp and put them to the test in order to judge their fitness for the Olympic team. On that day each man will put forward his supreme effort. Suddenly, to their astonishment, they learn that they have already been judged. Unknown to them, the super-athlete has been watching them all the time, measuring them by standards which have already been established. That's how we are to think of Paul's word to the Athenians about God having "fixed a day on which he will judge the world in righteousness by a man whom he has appointed". We needn't wait any longer. The judgment has taken place, the standard has been established, and we are continually being judged by it.

That's what makes the so-called "New Morality" so ridiculous, apart from the fact that it is not new and not always moral. We call it "situational", but it is really sentimental, simplistic and non-situational because it never faces up to the concrete situation. The key-word of the New Morality is "love". You do what *you* decide is the "loving thing" in every situation – like the doctor's son who forged his father's name on prescriptions to obtain drugs for his girl friend and pawned his mother's diamond ring to pay for them and felt no sense of wrong-doing, because it seemed to him the loving thing to do in that situation. The New

Morality tells you, as it told Adam and Eve, to take your place alongside God as the arbiter of good and evil and to write your own rules. So declared a theatre-owner in Toronto when the police charged him with showing obscene motion pictures. He said that profanity and obscenity are now acceptable in our society. They are "moral"; we write our own rules. He ignores the fact that the rules were written a long time ago and that we are continually being judged by them.

Some of us were on a pilgrimage to the Holy Land. When we came to a mountain beside the Sea of Galilee, one of the members of our party, a psychiatrist, conducted a worship service based on the Beatitudes. He shared with us his conviction that most mental disorders arise out of wrong relationships. He said that, in the light of his long experience as a practitioner of psychological medicine, he believed that the Beatitudes, enunciated on that very mountain, contain the highest wisdom ever given for achieving right relationships. He went through them one by one – poverty of spirit, meekness, mercy, purity of heart, etc.[10] – showing us that these are the practical, concrete, situational expressions of that right relationship of love which alone brings us complete health of personality. "But this is still a new teaching," he said. "Most of my patients have not even heard of it or, if they have heard of it, they have never seriously put it to work in their lives. This is the real new morality."

By that morality we are continually being judged. It is the plumb line[11] that God sets in the midst of his people to test the structures of their personal and corporate lives. If those structures sag, for whatever reason, their deviation is inexorably judged by the plumb line. That is why judgment remains an essential part of the Church's message to the world. The Church itself must not be judgmental because the Church is a fallible human institution and, as such, may be torn apart by a conflict of conscience. We see one example in the attitude of Christians to violence, some of whom regard violence under any pretext as an undiluted evil, while others acknowledge a Christian duty to correct injustice with force. By itself the Church is not corporately competent to judge the complicated structures of science, business, culture, politics and diplomacy, but the Church can proclaim the Word of God and allow that Word to exercise its own judgment. The Church's task is to remind men that God's judgment has taken place on the Cross of Christ, the standard has been established, and we are continually being judged by it.

IV

It is still a fair question to ask – Will there be a Last Judgment? Will there be a Judgment Day like that suggested by Paul in his sermon to the Athenians, and suggested by Jesus in many of his teachings, notably the parables of the Tares[12] and the Sheep and Goats[13]? If we want to retain an honest relationship to the New Testament and to the body of Christian doctrine we must assert with the Apostles' Creed, "From thence he shall come to judge the quick and the dead", and sing in the words of the Te Deum, "We believe that thou shalt come to be our Judge." The details of a Last Judgment may indeed make our imagination boggle, but the principle behind it calls to our reason. That principle is the outworking of God's justice. If God is a just, holy and righteous God, if he has truly revealed himself in Christ, only that which can live in the light of Christ's holiness will live in God's world eternally. There has to be some ultimate judgment of evil, some ultimate vindication of good.

Suppose we take the venture of faith and accept at face-value Paul's statement that God "has fixed a day on which he will judge the world in righteousness by a man whom he has appointed"? Suppose we dare to believe that there will be a Last Great Judgment at the end of history, what will it be like? According to the New Testament it will be the most surprising event in all eternity. A medieval monk said that everyone who makes it to heaven will be surprised by three things. First, he will be surprised to see a great many people whom he did not think would be there. Second, he will be surprised that some are not there whom he expected to see. Third, he will be surprised that he himself is there.

Jesus repeatedly warned that the Kingdom of God will be full of surprises. He told the scribes and Pharisees that tax collectors and harlots would go into the Kingdom ahead of them,[14] while many of his own followers might not get into the Kingdom

G

at all.[15] He said that the final separation of good and evil will be made in a way completely different from that which we permit ourselves to imagine. Not great achievements in the eyes of the world, not large professions of piety but small, simple things like feeding the hungry, clothing the naked and visiting the sick will be the criteria that decide our eternal destiny.[16] It will be a very surprising judgment.

It will also be a merciful judgment, simply because in the last analysis we shall be judged not by moral principles but by a merciful Judge. Dostoyevsky in his *Crime and Punishment* puts that truth on the lips of a drunk who pours out his misery to a tavern keeper:

"Why am I to be pitied, you say? Yes! There's nothing to pity me for! I ought to be crucified, crucified on a cross, not pitied! Crucify me, O judge, crucify me but pity me! ... He will pity us who has had pity on all men, who has understood all men and all things, He is the One, He too is the judge ... And He will judge and will forgive all, the good and the evil, the wise and the meek ... And when He has done with all of them, then He will summon us. 'You too come forth', He will say. 'Come forth, ye drunkards, come forth, ye weak ones, come forth, ye children of shame!' And we shall all come forth, without shame and shall stand before Him. And He will say unto us: 'Ye are swine made in the Image of the Beast and with his mark; but come ye also!' And the wise ones and those of understanding will say: 'O Lord, why dost Thou receive these men?' and He will say: 'This is why I receive them, O ye wise, this is why I receive them, O ye of understanding, that not one of them believed himself to be worthy of this.' And He will hold out His hands to us and we shall fall down before Him ... and we shall weep ... and we shall understand all things! ..."

It all goes back to the Cross. On Good Friday God judged the world in righteousness by the man whom he had appointed. He judges the crucifiers and He judges us whom they represent. But see what actually happens on Good Friday. The Divine Judge, having found us guilty and having sentenced us, does a strange thing. He steps down from the bench and stands beside us in the prisoner's dock, ready to suffer with us and for us and to take upon himself the full penalty of our crime. He the Judge offers himself to be judged in our place. That is what makes Christianity a Gospel. That is what makes the Word of God's Judgment a Word of God's Grace.

CHAPTER NOTES

1 Actually Congress refused two of the President's nominees. The third and successful nominee, Judge Harry A. Blackmun, was described by the American Civil Liberties Union as a man with "a capacity for objectivity and fairness in the highest degree, combined with a high intellect and a sharply honed legal mind".
2 John 8:11.
3 Matthew 23:27 R.S.V.
4 Mark 11:17 R.S.V.
5 Luke 22:61–62.
6 Luke 5:8 R.S.V.
7 John 8:12.
8 John 1:5 R.S.V.
9 Mary Bosanquet, *The Life and Death of Dietrich Bonhoeffer* (Hodder and Stoughton, London, 1968), p. 102.
10 Matthew 5:1 ff.
11 Amos 7:8.
12 Matthew 13:24–43.
13 Matthew 25:31–46.
14 Matthew 21:31.
15 Matthew 7:21–23.
16 Matthew 25:31–46.

CHAPTER SEVEN

Did Jesus Rise from the Dead?

"Now when they heard of the resurrection of the dead,
some mocked..."   *Acts* 17:32 R.S.V.

I want to make an outlandish proposition. In 1953 a party of British climbers conquered the summit of Mount Everest. It happened on the eve of the Queen's Coronation, almost as a gift to Her Majesty, and as such it heightened the sense of jubilation which everybody felt. I want to propose that *the event never happened at all.* The whole thing was staged and the whole story cleverly concocted for the prestige it would give the British Commonwealth throughout the world. The timing was brilliant, and it makes a good story, but it never really happened.

"Fantastic!" you say. Possibly, but no more fantastic than the reaction of many people to Easter. On Easter Day we Christians recall a far more significant victory than the conquest of Mount Everest. We celebrate the conquest of death in the resurrection of Jesus Christ from the tomb in Joseph's garden. Yet, ever since Paul preached to the Athenian philosophers on Mars Hill, men outside the Church have mocked at the idea of Christ's resurrection. Some have suspected it to be a plot cleverly contrived to raise the Church's morale. Even within the Church today there are men of considerable influence who are prepared to propose that the event never happened at all – at least in a physical and historical sense. The whole thing, they tell us, is a sacred myth and is commonly accepted as such by people of any intelligence. In a magazine interview one of the avant garde theologians in the United States declared quite seriously that he did not know a single theologian in his country who believes that Jesus rose from the dead. He corrected himself and said, "Yes, there is one, I believe – R. Niebuhr who is committed to the reality of the resurrection." He added confidently, "You know, he is the only one I can think of who is in this position in the whole country."[1] Obviously that settles the matter for the young "liberal". Does it settle the matter for us? Did Jesus rise from the dead?

I

Suppose I persist in the fantastic proposition that the successful assault on Everest was a myth concocted to raise public morale. If you take me seriously you will suggest that I try to be open-minded and look dispassionately at the facts of the case. At the very least I ought to consult the witnesses, the men who were there, who made the assault and whose first-hand testimony most sensible people accept. Exactly! And that's what we have to do if we seriously want an answer to the question, did Jesus rise from the dead? We must consult the witnesses, the men and women who saw Jesus or claimed to see him alive after he had been pronounced dead and buried in the tomb. Actually they number several hundred, but the time allows us to call only a few of them and listen to their first-hand testimony.

Mary Magdalene, what do you have to say? Mary answers: "Some of us went to the garden early in the morning on the first day of the week. We carried spices, hoping the soldiers would let us into the tomb to anoint the body of our Lord, but we found the place deserted, the stone rolled away, and the sepulchre empty. Thinking that someone had stolen the body, I went outside and threw myself on the ground and wept. A man approached. I thought he was the gardener, so I told him what had happened, He just said 'Mary', and I knew that it was Jesus."[2]

Let's listen to Cleopas: "Two of us were walking home to Emmaus after the Sabbath. A stranger caught up with us and asked why we were sad. We told him about Jesus, how he had been crucified and how we were mistaken in thinking him to be the Messiah. The stranger explained to us from the Scriptures how it was written that the Christ would have to suffer and die in order to save men. That comforted us and helped us to see things differently, so, when we reached our home in Emmaus, we invited him in for a meal. At the table he took bread and broke it, and immediately we recognised the stranger as Jesus."[3]

John, let us hear your story. "We were frightened after the crucifixion so we hid in the upper room and locked the door. I told the others about the sepulchre being empty, but that only frightened them more. Suddenly Jesus stood in our midst. We thought it was a ghost, coming through barred doors like that. But he talked with us and ate with us and gave us his blessing, and we believed."[4]

Thomas? "I was absent from the upper room when Jesus appeared there for the first time and I found it difficult to believe what the others, all ten of them, told me afterwards. But Jesus made me ashamed of my unbelief. He came again to the upper room, for my benefit, and allowed me to touch his wounded feet and hands and side. How could I doubt then?"[5]

What about you, Peter? "Well, I also doubted, even inside the empty sepulchre, but I was in the upper room on both occasions when the Risen Lord appeared there. I saw him again up in Galilee. It was on the lakeshore after we had been out fishing for the night. Three times, remembering how I had disgracefully denied him three times, he asked me the searching question, 'Simon, son of John, do you love me?' It was an experience that I shall never forget."[6]

Someone may protest, "But these witnesses are all biased. Like the men in the Everest party they could all have been involved in the plot. They believed in Jesus to begin with, so naturally they wanted to believe that he rose from the dead. Let's hear what a few neutral observers have to say." The truth is that there were no neutral observers at Easter, just as there were none at Everest, and if there had been any, do you think they would have believed what they saw? Do you think they would have recognised the risen Christ? Even the disciples did not recognise him at first. They mistook him for a gardener, a stranger, a ghost. He had to identify himself, call them by name, perform some familiar gesture, show them the wounds in his hands and side. So don't accuse them of wishful thinking, much less of hatching a plot. The fact is that the disciples did not expect Jesus to rise from the dead. Even though he had promised to return to them, they did not take his promise seriously, and when he did return, they still had to be convinced.

G. K. Chesterton once wrote: "If a dozen honest men tell me they have climbed the Matterhorn, I am satisfied that the summit is accessible, though I may never get there myself." We can never get back to the first Easter but we do know that more than a dozen honest men and women are willing to swear that they saw Jesus alive after he had been pronounced dead. So if the testimony of first-hand witnesses means anything, if we can believe that those who actually climbed the summit of the first Easter are telling the truth and not lying, maybe we can believe that Jesus Christ rose from the dead.

II

Suppose for some reason I persist in my argument that the successful assault on Everest was a cleverly contrived fake? What will you do next to dispel my stubborn scepticism? You will advise me to consult the records, the diary of Sir John Hunt and the photographs taken by Hillary and Tensing when they reached the summit. There *were* photographs – not like the cartoon which showed the two climbers planting a flag on a high mountain peak and each saying to the other, "But I thought *you* were supposed to bring the camera." Consult the records. Exactly! And we must put the event of Easter to the same test before we make up our minds whether or not it actually happened.

Let's wait a moment before looking at the Gospel stories which, after all, were oral traditions written down several years after the event and which differ somewhat in their details – though that very fact may increase their reliability. If all told precisely the same story, with no variations, then we might have good reason to suspect that clever men had put their heads together and made it up. Look first, however, at the earliest Christian records in the Book of Acts. One of the first acts of the apostles, after Jesus left them, was to elect a successor to Judas, the betrayer, who had committed suicide.[7] The candidate must have one qualification above all others: he must be a witness to the Resurrection, a man who had seen the Risen Christ. That made him an apostle. So, right away the Christian Church attached first importance, not to the life or teachings or even the death of Jesus but to God's mighty act in raising him from the dead. We have only to read the earliest Christian sermons, recorded in the Book of Acts, all of which proclaim a single theme. Peter announced it on the Day of Pentecost: "This Jesus God raised up, and of that we are all witnesses."[8]

Look at Paul's New Testament Letters, which pre-date the written Gospels, especially his First Letter to the Christians in Corinth. Corinth was a wide-open seaport city in southern Greece, notorious throughout the ancient world as a hotbed of prostitutes, drunkards, perverts, thieves and racketeers. Yet within a few years of the Crucifixion the Apostle Paul established a flourishing Church there, and within that Church were to be found men and women leading lives of astonishing purity and goodness. What produced this marvellous change of character? Paul says that it was the Gospel, and he defines this transforming Gospel in the fifteenth chapter:

"For I delivered to you as of first importance what I also received, that Christ died for our sins in accordance with the scriptures, that he was buried, that he was raised on the third day in accordance with the scriptures, and that he appeared to Cephas, then to the twelve. Then he appeared to more than five hundred brethren at one time, most of whom are still alive, though some have fallen asleep. Then he appeared to James, then to all the apostles. Last of all, as to one untimely born, he appeared also to me . . ."[9]

Those words were written before any of the Gospel stories and they were written to Greeks by an intellectual giant who himself was a product of Greek culture. Regarded by scholars as one of the earliest and most reliable pieces of historical writing in the New Testament, they assert a single fact, viz. that Jesus Christ rose from the dead.

An eminent British lawyer, Sir Edwin Clarke, has said:

"I have made a prolonged study of the evidence for the events of the first Easter Day. To me the evidence is conclusive. Over and over again in High Court I have secured a verdict on evidence not nearly so compelling. Inference follows on evidence, and a truthful witness is always artless and disdains effect. The Gospel evidence for the Resurrection is of this class, and as a lawyer I accept it unreservedly as the testimony of truthful men to fact they were able to substantiate."[10]

With that strong statement in mind let us consider the evidence in the Gospel records. As Sir Edwin Clarke suggests, its very artlessness reduces to absurdity the charge that it is a conspiracy of lies. Naturally the return of Christ from the dead, like the return of any man from the dead, made a tremendous emotional impact on those who witnessed it first-hand; but remember that the Gospel writers, who listened to this witness and later wrote it down, were writing with a profound respect for truth. No one would sift the evidence more carefully than Luke, the Greek doctor who was also, even by modern standards, a professional historian, and it is he who gives the most detailed account of the first Easter Day.[11] It begins with the early morning visit of the women to the empty tomb and the vision of angels who tell them that Christ is risen, a story which the disciples toss off as "an idle tale". Then comes the afternoon journey to Emmaus and the revelation of the Risen Christ to his two sorrowing friends who immediately rush back to Jerusalem to tell the good news to the disciples in the upper room. That evening Christ himself suddenly appears in the upper room, so suddenly that the disciples think him a ghost, and he does some astonishing things – allows them to touch his body, shows them the wounds of his crucifixion and even asks them for food. Who ever heard of a ghost *eating*? Remember that Luke begins his Gospel by stating his intention to write an accurate history. Would it not be strange, therefore, if he brought it all to a climax with a myth? Luke, the historian, certainly accepted the evidence that Jesus rose from the dead.

About the time when our more liberal thinkers were beginning to explain the Resurrection stories as a sacred myth, J. B. Phillips wrote an article expressing his concern over the effect of this avant-garde theology on ordinary people. Phillips is no reactionary. He is one of the most popular, adventurous and exciting of modern translators of the New Testament. No man has worked more closely with the records and no man is more competent to tell the difference between fact and fiction. In this article Phillips says that after many years of translating the Bible there has grown within him a respect amounting to awe for the material on which he was working. He says that with very few exceptions he felt that he was dealing with the real genuine stuff. He ends his article by saying: "With all the emphasis that I can command I must set down my strong and enduring impression from close study of the New Testament that this miracle (the Resurrection) really happened. Jesus Christ did rise from the dead."[12]

III

So now some chinks are beginning to appear in the armour of my stubborn resistance. I admit that the British expedition may possibly have climbed Mount Everest but I still feel a niggling doubt because I wasn't there when it happened. Obviously you cannot provide a time-machine that will take me back nearly twenty years ago to India but you can suggest that, after hearing the witnesses and consulting the records, I take one more thing into account. If Hillary, Hunt and Co. made it all up, they have missed their true calling. They are superb actors and should be making a fortune on the stage. Whatever they said, they certainly acted like men who had conquered the summit. Their manner and bearing, their exuberant spirit and the light of victory in their eyes bore far more eloquent testimony than mere words. Exactly! We cannot board a time-machine and go back two thousand years to ancient Palestine and be present on the first Easter Day but we can take a good look at some of the men and women who *were* present on the first Easter day. Whatever they said about Christ rising from the dead, they certainly behaved as though Christ had risen from the dead. And this is surely the most powerful argument for the Resurrection – the difference it made to the disciples.

It was nothing less than the difference between life and death. The disciples died with Jesus on Calvary. Their bodies still moved, but they were like walking corpses, because when they saw his corpse taken down from the Cross, their souls shrivelled up and died. Suddenly they came to life again, and the reason, they said, was that Christ had come to life again. Doubt the witness of their tongues, if you will, but you cannot doubt the witness of their lives. Something happened to those confused, fear-stricken, heart-broken disciples on the third day after their Lord's Crucifixion. Something restored their faith and kept it alive in the face of suffering, persecution and martyrdom. Something restored their hope and kept it alive when the world made mockery of their dreams. Something restored their love and kept it alive when all men hated them and called them fools. Something restored their zeal for Christ's Kingdom and kept alive, until the Church of the Upper Room became the Church of the four corners of the earth.

At this point someone will surely say, Isn't there a simple explanation to this remarkable change in the disciples? They had recovered from their sense of grief at losing Jesus and now felt the inspiration of his memory. Every great man, when he dies, leaves something of himself behind and, if he has been great enough, his influence will live on and inspire other men to serve his ideals. They may even think and speak of him as though he were still alive. Visitors to Washington are always impressed by the Lincoln Memorial. When you stand inside that white marble shrine and gaze at the massive, life-like statue and read the words of the immortal Gettysburg Address carved on the wall, you feel a presence which tells you that Lincoln is still very much alive. Death did not obliterate this great human personality. Wherever people honour God, revere simplicity, love their fellow-men and give themselves unsparingly for justice, freedom and equality, wherever men consciously serve the ideals of Lincoln, the spirit of Lincoln lives on. Is it not possible that Jesus made the same impact on the disciples so that, after recovering from the initial shock of bereavement, they took hold of themselves and, realising the greatness of what he had lived and died for, dedicated themselves to carry on his work? Would that not explain their own change of heart and would it not explain their belief that Christ had risen from the dead?

It might, except for one thing (apart from the fact that people don't usually recover from bereavement in three days). By human standards Jesus was not a great man, not nearly as great as Abraham Lincoln. He didn't write books or hold office in Church or state. We can say, without being dogmatic, that if Jesus had depended for immortality on the scope and significance of his earthly career, his influence would not have survived at all. That career lasted only a year and a half and was quite unnoticed except by a few peasants in a remote corner of the Roman Empire and by a few minor officials who quickly snuffed it out like a candle. The curtain that fell on the Good Friday drama fell also on the earthly career of Jesus and on the faith and hopes of the men who had trusted and followed him. Do you seriously believe that a mere awakening of memory would account for the manner and bearing, the exuberant spirit and the light of victory that people saw in the eyes of the disciples after Easter? What you have to account for is a company of men so on fire with a passion for Christ's Kingdom that they went out in the face of all opposition and danger to turn the world upside down and change the course of history. You have to account for the New Testament, the Church, the saints, the martyrs, the missionaries – a religious movement so inherently dynamic that it spans the centuries and girdles the globe. No human personality, even one so powerful as Jesus, could have produced all of this. It needed an act of God, an act as earth-shaking, history-making and soul-transforming as the Resurrection of Jesus Christ from the dead.

It is all very interesting and perhaps convincing, but does it matter if we can prove that Jesus Christ rose from the dead? The ascent of Mount Everest may have raised public morale but it really wasn't important. It made no appreciable difference to our lives or to the life of the world. Is the Empty Tomb any more important? Paul answers that question. *He* makes the proposition that Jesus did not rise from the dead and he faces the implications squarely, honestly and fearlessly. Writing to the Corinthians he says, "If Christ has not been raised, your faith is futile and you are still in your sins. Then those also who have fallen asleep in Christ are perished."[18] Paul is saying that, if the event of the Resurrection did not actually happen, then the Church is based on a monstrous lie. Evil will have the last word in this world, and man will be defeated because God has been defeated. As far as we know, death will be the end of us, because we have no reason for hope beyond the grave. A former Bishop of London commented most eloquently on Paul's words when he told of an argument between two scholars. One of them said, "The Empty Tomb does not matter." The other replied, "Remove the Empty Tomb from Christianity, and we have nothing left."

CHAPTER NOTES

1   An interview with T. Altizer reported in the *New Christian*, March 7, 1968, p. 13.
2   John 20:11–18.
3   Luke 24:13–35.
4   John 20:1–10, 19–23.
5   John 20:24–29.
6   John 21:1 ff.
7   Acts 1:15–26.
8   Acts 2:32 R.S.V.
9   I Cor. 15:3–8 R.S.V.
10 Quoted in the *Expository Times*, March 1967, pp. 186–7.
11 Luke 24:1 ff.
12 Reported in the *Church Times*, June 18, 1965.
13 I Cor. 15:17–18.

CHAPTER EIGHT

The Centrality of Preaching

The Verdict

A few years ago I guided a party of pilgrims on a tour of the Holy Land. On our return journey we stopped for a day at Athens, long enough to visit the Acropolis, the ruined glory of a bygone age. Under the shadow of the towering Parthenon is a mound of rock formerly known as the Areopagus, or Mars Hill, where the inquisitive Athenians regularly assembled to hear speakers and lecturers, the professional pedlars of new ideas. Steps led up to the summit of this rock. Fixed in the wall beside them is a bronze plaque inscribed with the Greek text of the one sermon which the Apostle Paul preached in this city and on this site. For a few moments we all sat silently on that mound of rock, trying to recreate in our minds the scene of that memorable occasion. Then I opened the New Testament and read aloud Paul's sermon from the seventeenth chapter of Acts. I found it a moving experience, as my party of Christian pilgrims listened with rapt attention. They were a congregation strikingly different from the one addressed by Paul nearly two thousand years ago.

We rember who those people were. They were Greek intellectuals lusting only to hear some "new thing" and unaware that they were, in fact, hearing about a new thing, the only radically new thing that God has done since the creation of the world. They did not recognise that they were listening to one of the greatest preachers of all time, one of the greatest sermons of all time, a sermon setting forth the mighty themes of God, Man, Judgment and Resurrection. "These Athenian Philosophers," writes Professor Pelikan, "did not recognize the truth in Christ because they had not found a Christ in truth." How did they react to Paul's preaching? What was their verdict? The New Testament tells us quite plainly: "... some mocked; but others said, 'We will hear you again about this'... But some men joined him and believed ..."

Every preacher encounters essentially the same three reactions among the people who listen to his sermons. There are still those who mock his preaching. You find scoffers in every congregation. They come to Church only out of habit or curiosity, their bias sticking out all over them like the quills on a porcupine. They have no intention of being convinced. They know the answers anyway, their minds are made up, and they don't want the preacher to confuse them with facts. Sermons only harden them in their resistance to the Gospel. "What did we tell you?" they murmur afterwards. "He has nothing to say, nothing new!" Or it may be that they do not scoff at preaching itself but only at the preaching of the *Gospel*. They are receptive enough to homiletic froth, to light, perfumed discourses which comfort them and build up their self-esteem. What they object to is the faithful exposition of sound doctrine. Every congregation abounds in clerical amateurs who have their own idea of what the man in the pulpit ought to say and who want him simply to boost their morale and confirm them in their own prejudices. Let the preacher speak to them of the deep things from God's Word, and they turn away from him in derision, exclaiming, "It's too much for me! He's over my head!"

You also find in every congregation the second group who react by saying, "We will hear you again about this," a reaction which may be interpreted in one of two ways. It may be nothing more than pious patronage, a polite brush-off, the kind of good intention that paves the road to hell and makes every preacher cringe. Some affluent member of the church, on an expense account, entertains you at his club where he introduces you to a jovial fellow who has just swallowed his third cocktail. This character greets you effusively by saying, "I have been wanting to meet you, Reverend. It may surprise you, but I dropped in at one of your services a few months ago, and I want to tell you that you preached a fine sermon, a damn fine sermon." Then he adds, as though he were conferring upon you, and upon God, the highest of all favours, "One of these Sundays I'm going to drop in and hear you again."

We hope, however, that among the Athenians who told Paul, "We will hear you again about this," there were those who really meant it. We assume that on Mars Hill there were some people who recognised that the Gospel which they had just heard was so radically new and of such magnitude that they could not expect to grasp its full implications within the space of one sermon. They must probe into it more deeply, consider it more carefully, and to that end they spoke sincerely when they told Paul that they wanted to hear him again. That is the most that any preacher can ask of a congregation – that they will hear him again, not just at some indefinite date in the vague future, but next Sunday, and the Sunday after, and the Sunday after that. Effective preaching does not try to communicate the whole Gospel in a single sermon. It comprises a man's total pulpit ministry as he takes his people through the seasons of the Church Year, rehearsing the mighty acts of God, expounding the great doctrines of the Faith and playing the searchlight of the Gospel on all the dark areas of personal and social life. Given that opportunity, his preaching cannot fail to bear some fruit.

That becomes possible, however, not only as a congregation stays with its minister but also as a minister stays with his people. No man ever becomes a great preacher who changes his pastorates too frequently like a bee buzzing from flower to flower, ever searching for something more sweet. Some years ago a classmate of mine in Canada, who had emigrated to an American denomination because it offered him better prospect of personal advancement, came home for a visit and boasted, "I have had three quick moves in three years." Apart from the hardship worked upon his family, what could he hope to accomplish for any congregation in these pastoral whistle-stops? What minister in his first few years at a church really says anything from the pulpit? He may repeat all the obvious truths which his predecessors have said before him and probably draws from his barrel of old sermons. Only when he has exhausted the usual themes and the familiar passages of Scripture and has begun to dig for himself does he bring forth treasures of the Gospel which have originality and power; only then does he speak with authority. The congregation itself in the first few years listens to his sermons. Gradually, within the solidifying framework of his pastoral relationship, they begin listening to him, to his Gospel and his total message. Because he is their shepherd and not a hireling, they know his voice and trust what he says. They do not know the voice of strangers, not even if the stranger be the most renowned pulpit giant in all Christendom.

Paul had a third group of hearers on Mars Hill of whom the historian writes, "But some joined him and believed." Paul left no flourishing church behind him in Athens but he did leave a few changed lives. The Bible mentions two of them by name: "Dionysius the Areopagite and a woman named Damaris." Their names do not recur in the New Testament. We have no idea what became of them, whether they remained steadfast in their new witness or lost their enthusiasm in the chilly atmosphere of intellectual pride. We only know that they responded actively to the preaching of the Gospel. Seekers for truth, they recognised in the proclamation of Christ the goal of their seeking. Here at last was Reality, that real world of which this world is only a kind of pale shadow. It might prove to be a mirage, but at least they would give it a chance; they would stake their lives upon it; they would take the venture of faith.

It is the supreme thrill of preaching that sometimes it does change lives, and a single sermon kindles fire in a heart that has grown cold. Every preacher every time he stands in the pulpit hopes and prays that within his congregation, slumped in the back pews perhaps, there may be some seeking souls who potentially belong to that small but vitally important third group on Mars Hill. What he has to say on that day speaks directly to their hearts. Something within them comes out to meet and respond to his sermon. Through the preacher's Word the living Christ confronts them, demanding a verdict, and they are glad to give it. That is what binds us to our vocation and justifies the ministry of preaching, as no egotistical or material considerations

113

could ever do. That is why the question, "Should we stop preaching?" must be answered with a resounding "No!"

The Foolishness of Preaching

Beyond any doubt the Church's preaching ministry has gone into an eclipse. Group dynamics, pastoral counselling, community outreach and a number of other cults stand like celestial bodies between the pulpit and the pew. Many factors in the Church and the world militate against preaching, with the result that, apart from stubborn exceptions, the Church is not producing pulpit men of the calibre produced a few generations ago. That does not worry the people who display a fashionable contempt for preaching and who disparagingly describe the sermon as an "ego-trip" or a "monologue". Of course, the sermon is not a monologue, not if there is a congregation present and not if God is present. An American evangelist says that he never preaches to less than five people – himself, one other person, God the Father, God the Son and God the Holy Spirit. Nevertheless there are those who believe quite sincerely that the whole posture of a giving preacher and a receiving congregation dehumanises the Church and is precisely the image which the Church has to change if it hopes to survive and be acceptable to the younger generation. They declare dogmatically that preaching is dead and that the only decent thing left to do is bury it.

Such people have a right to speak for themselves, but only for themselves. Their kind of preaching may be dead, and perhaps they ought to bury it; but let them not impose their own moribundity on the whole Church. In some places preaching is still very much alive. Every Sunday in Hamburg, Germany, Dr. Helmut Thielicke preaches to congregations, mainly of university students, that number in the thousands. He suggests that the disparagement of preaching and its displacement by other forms of communication may, in fact, be a form of escape from the discipline and hard work that preaching involves. He is quoted by Elton Trueblood in his book, *The Incendiary Fellowship*, who gives his opinion that men who derogate preaching are for the most part precisely those who cannot do it well. That is certainly a strange reversal of thought for the Quaker philosopher and great exponent of lay religion who for years has been trying to break down the barrier between pulpit and pew. Trueblood, however, can read the signs of the times. He knows that in every generation the Church has peculiar needs and he believes that in this generation the time has come for the Church to put greater stress upon the professional ministry and on vital preaching.[1]

Let it be the purpose of this final lecture not only to encourage the continuance of the preaching ministry but to emphasise its centrality in the Church's life. Let us insist that the throne of Protestantism is still the pulpit, that the climax of public worship is the sermon and that the spoken word of a preacher is still the most effective means of proclaiming the Word of God. We take the Apostle Paul as our authority. The meagre response of his hearers on Mars Hill did not discourage him as a preacher. He didn't move on to Corinth, disgruntled and muttering to himself, "I guess I'd better quit preaching and experiment with other ways of communicating the Gospel." Paul judged his vocation not by those who failed to respond but by those who did respond. He knew well enough that there are times when preaching seems futile and foolish, but he knew also that the foolishness of God is wiser than the wisdom of men. Thus he would write to the Corinthians, "It pleased God by the foolishness of preaching to save them that believe" (I Cor. 1:21). Four factors lie at the basis of that claim.

THE THEOLOGICAL FACTOR

First, the theological factor. We have to keep reminding ourselves that Christianity is an historical religion. It started with an event which brought to a climax seventeen centuries of sacred history and itself changed the history of the world. That event was the birth in Bethlehem of a baby in whom dwelt all the fullness of the eternal God. The writer of the fourth Gospel expressed the truth of the Incarnation in this way: "The Word became flesh and dwelt among us, full of grace and truth." (John 1:14) God has a Word, as you and I have words, a language of communicating and dealing with people, a means of self-expression. Sometimes we speak our words, sometimes we write them, just as God spoke through the prophets and wrote on the pages of nature and history. Then God *did* something, something that only God can do: he made his Word not only audible but visible. At a fixed point in history and at a fixed place upon the earth's surface God clothed his eternal Word in the human flesh of Jesus of Nazareth. Jesus did not merely speak the Word of God; he was the Word of God. This miracle of miracles, this Christ-event, is the foundation on which the whole structure of Christianity rests.

An event cannot take place in a vacuum. If Jesus had been born on the summit of Mount Everest or spent his life as a recluse in the Sahara Desert, the Incarnation would have been a waste of human and divine energy. What gives the Word-made-flesh the character of an event is the fact that it took place among people who experienced it and reacted to it and witnessed to it and committed their witness to writing. Without that writing, which has come down to us in Scripture, the Incarnation would, as Emil Brunner says, "have echoed like a sound which passes unheard in a primeval forest. It would have been like a bridge which had been begun from one side of a river but which had never reached the other side." There is no revelation of God in Christ apart from the prophetic witness in the Old Testament and the apostolic witness in the New Testament. Scripture not only records the Christ-event; it is a constitutive part of the Christ-event. The Bible does more than witness to the Word of God; in a very real sense the Bible is the Word of God.

The event does not stop there. It continues in so far as the Word of God, made visible in Jesus and contained in the Bible, is related, proclaimed and interpreted from the pulpit. As Paul says, "How are men to call upon him in whom they have not believed? And how are they to believe in him of whom they have never heard? And how are they to hear without a preacher?" (Rom. 10:14). To be sure, not everything that goes by the name of preaching can qualify as a faithful proclamation of the Word of God, but preaching that is true preaching does more than convey the good news of the Christ-event; it is part of the event itself. Indeed, Christianity is unique among all religions in that preaching does not merely propagate the Faith but is itself a constitutive element of the Faith. No liturgy, not even the Lord's

Supper, can displace the sermon as the central and effective means of prolonging the Event of the Incarnation.

The words of Karl Barth should be framed and displayed on the wall of every minister's study. We quote them again:

> "On Sunday morning when the bells ring to call the congregation and minister to church, there is in the air an *expectancy* that something great, crucial and even momentous is to happen ... And here above all is a *man*, upon whom the expectation of the apparently imminent event seems to rest in a special way ... He will open the *Bible* and read from it words of infinite import, words that refer, all of them, to God. And then he will enter the pulpit and – here is daring! – *preach;* that is, he will add to what has been read from the Bible something from his own head and heart ..."[2]

Rightly Barth has been designated by our generation as the theologian of the Word of God, the Word in its threefold manifestation through Christ, through the Bible and through pulpit proclamation. Some of our liturgical liberals would like to eliminate the sermon and make the public worship of God a "happening". The sermon, as Barth sees it, *is* a "happening". Something does happen when a preacher takes the inspired truths of Holy Scripture, passes them through the prism of his own mind and with them lights up the dark places in the lives of his people. Preaching at its best is a sacrament. That same eternal Word of God, who became flesh in Jesus of Nazareth and to whom the written words of Scripture bear witness, confronts the people of God through the spoken word of his prophet. That is the theological basis for preaching and that is why Paul confidently declared that "it pleased God through the foolishness of preaching to save them that believe."

HISTORY

Look at history as a second factor in the centrality of preaching. Not for a moment do we deprecate the other ordinances of public worship, though curiously enough we read little about them in the Bible. So far as liturgy is concerned, God seems to have grown rather bored with it at times: "Your new moons and your appointed feasts my soul hates; they have become a burden to me, I am weary of bearing them." (Isaiah 1:14). In Old Testament days, when God really wanted to open a channel of communication and bind the people more closely to his will, he invariably did it through the voice of a prophet who declared, "The Word of the Lord came unto me, saying..."

Did not Jesus himself stand in the prophetic tradition? The first thing written of him, as he entered upon his public ministry, was that he "came into Galilee preaching the Gospel of God" (Mark 1:14). The people acclaimed him as a prophet. When he made his triumphal entry into Jerusalem on Palm Sunday, so that the whole city was stirred, saying, "Who is this?", the crowds replied, "This is the prophet Jesus from Nazareth of Galilee." (Matt. 21:11) Men listened to Jesus because he spoke for God and spoke with authority, not as the scribes. Like his prophetic predecessors Jesus looked with suspicion on the ritualism of temple worship, not for its own sake but because it mesmerised people and because it bore no relation to the moral realities of their personal and corporate lives.

When we consider the Church's preaching ministry we do well to remember that, by the power of the Holy Spirit, the preaching of the first apostles brought the Church into being. To be sure, Christian believers themselves assembled together to dramatise the Incarnate Word in a sacramental meal, but it was the *spoken* word that made the Church into the witness society that Christ commissioned it to be. After the Risen Christ had departed from their sight, the disciples set out to tell people about him. They preached so powerfully that in a single day, as a re-result of one man's sermon, three thousand souls were added to the Church (Acts 2:41). We have seen that Paul was primarily a preacher. To whatever city he came in the Mediterranean world he went on the Sabbath Day into the synagogue and to an assembled congregation of Jews and Gentiles told the story of salvation, the Good News that in the life and death and resurrection of Jesus Christ God had visited and redeemed his people.

It might be interesting to note by way of parenthesis that Paul had something to say about the experience of liturgical ecstasy which some of our modern communicators would like to see in place of the sermon. Apparently it is no new phenomenon in Christian worship. Paul writes about it at some length in the fourteenth chapter of First Corinthians, a chapter which the modern communicators have seemingly not read. Paul does not criticise liturgical ecstasy for its own sake; he simply says that it has no permanent results, no power to build up the Church. He compares it to the senseless, cacophonous music such as we hear in the sound tracks of science-fiction movies – impressive music but not a clear trumpet-call to battle. He suggests that if some unbelievers or uninstructed persons suddenly broke in on us while we are engaged in one of these psychedelic jags, they would think that we were mad. And he states his own position by saying, "I would rather speak five intelligible words, for the benefit of others as well as myself, than thousands of words in the language of ecstasy." (I Cor. 14:19).

Look back into history and see how many of the great revivals and reformations of religion have come to pass through preaching. The awakening of faith is indissolubly linked to this vibrant and vital witness. In his book, *Preaching Unashamed*, Joseph Sizoo reminds us that "when Isaiah stood up to preach, a whole new concept of holiness was born in the earth. When Jeremiah walked out of the fields of Anathoth to prophesy, a new morality came to a whole nation. When Amos left his plough in the furrows of Tekoa and began to preach, there emerged a new social justice. When Augustine proclaimed the Holy City, there came with it the dawn of a new conscience. When Francis went up and down the village streets preaching, there came a new compassion for the poor and underprivileged. Through the preaching of Luther there blossomed in the earth a spiritual emancipation. The preaching of Calvin brought into being the birth of modern democracy. Through the preaching of John Wesley there was ushered in the age of the common man."[3]

Such is the witness of history. A new day dawns for the world when from among the faithful remnant God raises up prophets whose words and lives proclaim the truth that is in Jesus Christ. If the story of our Faith teaches us anything it is this – "It pleased

God through the foolishness of preaching to save them that believe."

Let us appeal to personal experience as a basis for our faith in the centrality of preaching. The Danish theologian Kierkegaard related a homely parable about a flock of geese that milled around in a filthy barnyard imprisoned by a high wooden fence. One day a preaching goose came into their midst. He stood on an old crate and admonished the geese for being content with their confined, earthbound existence. He recounted the exploits of their forefathers who spread their wings and flew the trackless wastes of the sky. He spoke of the goodness of the Creator who had given geese the urge to migrate and the wings to fly. This pleased the geese. They nodded their heads and marvelled at these things and applauded the eloquence of the preaching goose. All this they did. But one thing they never did; they did not fly. They went back to their waiting dinner, for the corn was good and the barnyard secure.

That's what discourages most preachers – not the sight of empty pews but the awareness that on Sunday mornings people listen to sermons, marvel at them, applaud them and even nod their heads in approval, then go back to their waiting dinners and their earthbound existence with no intention of spreading their wings and soaring to the heights of spiritual reality. How many sermons does a man preach in forty years of ministry? Say 2,000. Allowing half an hour per sermon, that's a lot of talking, but what does it all accomplish beyond filling the air with pleasing or displeasing rhetoric? How many lives does it change? How many broken bodies and souls does it heal? How many people does it reconcile to God? Surveying the situation honestly, the preacher cannot be blamed for entering his pulpit with a certain sense of futility, suspecting that Paul may have coined exactly the right phrase when he wrote about "the foolishness of preaching".

In one of his books, Henry Sloane Coffin suggests that the major discouragement of many a hard-working minister who puts study, thought, painstaking writing and sincere prayer into the composition of his sermons is the haunting question, "What comes of it all?" It is, in fact, the seeming futility and foolishness of preaching that takes the heart out of many a conscientious ambassador for Christ and tempts him to opt out of the pulpit ministry. He sees his friends and acquaintances in various businesses and professions achieving measurable gains. Doctors and social workers can help people in a tangible way, but how intangible at best are the results of preaching! Few of us ever know whether anything we have said from the pulpit has ever produced a single spiritual consequence. Then Dr. Coffin conveys a word of extreme encouragement. He tells us of something that Canon Twells, the writer of the beautiful hymn, "At even e'er the sun was set," once said in the formal language of devout Victorians; and we can do no better than quote his words:

"A friend of mine, a layman, was in the company of an eminent preacher, then in the decline of life. My friend happened to remark what a comfort it must be to think of all the good he had done by his gift of eloquence. The eyes of the old man filled with tears: 'You little know. You little know. If I ever turned one heart from the ways of disobedience to the wisdom of the just, God has withheld the assurance from me. I have been admired and run after and flattered; but how gladly would I forget all that, to be told of one single soul I have been instrumental in saving!' The eminent preacher entered into his rest." And Twells continues. "There was a great funeral. Many passed around the grave who had often hung on his lips. My friend was there, and by his side was a stranger who was so deeply moved that when it was over my friend said to him, 'You knew him, I suppose.' 'Knew him?' came the reply. 'No, I never spoke to him; but I owe him my soul.' "[4]

There are people who will say the same thing about all of us, though they may not have the courage to say it to our faces. Not that we have reason to boast, for we know ourselves to be but earthen vessels; and if our pulpit ministry bears any visible fruit at all, we shall give the glory to God. Yet it is a poor preacher indeed who does not cherish at least a few memories that encourage and sustain him in the pursuit of his vocation. From my own experience I take the liberty of sharing one such memory.

Not long ago I received a letter from a magnificent Christian telling me that after a lingering and painful illness his wife had died of cancer. I dare not quote the entire letter, because that be admitting you into the most intimate and sacred shrine of his personality, but I can tell you that it witnessed to a great triumph of faith as he and his beloved wife and their teenage son accepted this tragedy together and said their farewells in full assurance of the love of God. In recent years this man has been a lay preacher and a stalwart leader in the Church, especially among young people, but it was not always so. For a long time, as a war veteran and as a mining engineer who travelled extensively, he remained indifferent to religion altogether. My first encounter with him was when he made an appointment and came to my vestry one evening, sat down on a chair and asked bluntly, "Where do I go from here?" Noticing my puzzled expression, he went on to explain that for several weeks he had been attending services in our church, but without any serious intention of introducing himself. Then he leaned forward and said, "Last Sunday you said something that hit me. You said 'Stop worrying about what you cannot accept of the Christian Faith and commit yourself to what you can accept.' So where do I go from here? How do I become a real Christian? How can I serve the Church?" That was more than ten years ago, and now in his Gethsemane of sorrow he writes a letter of which, perhaps, he would permit me to quote two sentences:

> "My reason for writing all of this is to say once more how eternally grateful I am to you for putting me back on the right track again, and to let you know that your preaching bears fruit and will, I hope, continue to do so. I think I have caught the faintest glimpse of how God, through Christ, can help us, because he has walked this way before."

Our own experience teaches us that "it pleased God by the foolishness of preaching to save them that believe".

The Centrality of Preaching

Consider the Church's mission as a basis for our faith in the centrality of preaching. The Church is the Body of Christ. Here on earth, at a place which can still be located, a date firmly fixed in history, the eternal Son of God clothed himself in our human flesh and began a ministry of reconciliation. After his Resurrection he committed that ministry to his disciples, promising to be among them eternally. As he had dwelt for a time in a flesh and blood body, so now he would dwell in a corporate body, the Church. "We have this ministry" (II Cor. 4:1), declared Paul, this same ministry of Christ. What Christ was to the world the Church must be to the world – the incarnate life of God committed to the ministry of reconciliation.

Need we remind ourselves again that Jesus began that ministry by preaching? He "came into Galilee preaching the Gospel of God"; and, when he bequeathed his ministry to the disciples, he specified preaching as their first and principal means of witness. "Go into all the world and preach the Gospel to the whole creation." (Mark 16:15) We preach, therefore, not because we want to preach or because we feel the inner compulsion to do so but because we have received a direct, divine mandate to preach. That mandate is a part of the original givenness of Christ himself, a constitutive part of the very event which God has accomplished for the world's salvation.

Not that preaching is the only form of Christian witness. In these days, when the Church is supposed to be "where the action is", the world may be more impressed by our deeds than by our words, and our strongest witness may be simply the evidence that we care. Christ conducted a caring ministry. He performed works of compassion and he authorised the disciples to perform them in his name. He also authorised them to preach. He did so because he knew that by itself a work of compassion may tell nothing about the saving power of God. It may cure men's bodies but leave their souls in a state of sickness. Healing, education and social service in Christ's name must be accompanied and interpreted by the preaching of the Gospel in order to communicate the power of God unto salvation. What impressed me most about the Edinburgh Medical Clinic in Nazareth, when I visited that mission hospital, was the fact that every day for more than a hundred years work has stopped between the hours of seven and seven-thirty in the evening while the doctors and nurses stand in the wards and tell the patients *why* they have come to heal them in the name of Christ. The Medical Superintendent told me, "We do not try to proselytise but we believe that we owe it to our patients to share with them the motives and inspiration of our service. We believe that every man has a right to hear the Gospel."

Every man has a right to hear the Gospel – that conviction brought the Church into being, it made us Christians, it has inspired the Church's mission all down the centuries, and it needs to be recovered today if the Church hopes to recover its ancient power. Whatever the experts in communication may tell us, I still believe that the spoken Word of God must command the central place in the Church's worship and the Church's evangelistic outreach. This is more crucial than we realise, simply because our generation has experienced in a new way the terrible potency of speech. Preaching is not dead; it has simply been expropriated. The volume of words communicated on any one Sunday from all the pulpits in Christendom is very small compared with the volume communicated seven days a week by radio and television into every home in the land. Today the ether is full of preaching, some of it uplifting, some of it blasphemous and a lot of it downright stupid.

In 1969 a religious journal in Canada conducted a nation-wide opinion poll to discover the names of the mass media communicators – broadcasters, lecturers, writers, journalists, editors – who exercise the greatest influence on popular thinking. The fourteen people named were invited to answer questionnaires. Four described themselves as atheists, four as agnostics, and here is a sampling of their specific answers: "I define God as my conscience." "Jesus was a deluded Jewish youth." "The effect of religion on man has been to keep him in line through fear of the unknown." "The Church is a nice little exercise in futility." "The purpose of existence is to exist." "After death, there is nothing." So say the spokesmen of our culture, the secular preachers who are preaching daily to hundreds of thousands of listeners and who are in a position to make a more powerful impact on popular thought than are all the spokesmen of God put together.

Yet, strangely enough, it was not the religious press but a secular daily newspaper, the Ottawa *Journal*, that recently gave strong support to preaching and sound advice to preachers. I was so heartened by it that I sent a telegram of appreciation which the editor acknowledged and published. The telegram read: "We have reached a sad state of affairs when a secular daily newspaper has to remind the Church of its priorities, yet we seem to have reached exactly that state. Lacking encouragement from some of our leaders and laymen, we preachers accept it most gratefully from the Ottawa *Journal*. Thank you."

On May 9th, 1970 the *Journal* published a lead editorial in which it disagreed sharply with Dr. Robert McClure, Moderator of the United Church of Canada, who had publicly expressed his view that sermons are on their way out, that large congregations are dying and will be replaced by "cells" of twelve families in an apartment block or community region which would gather together under a volunteer leader to pursue their worship according to their common interests and experiences. He gave as the reason: "We are coming to a time and level of intelligence when a minister can no longer gauge a sermon of universal use. The effect is heroic but useless." The *Journal* expressed concern that religion reduced to the convenience of a coffee party might lose its soul but it was even more concerned with the Moderator's requiem for preaching. It said:

".... If Dr. McClure's world is attaining a level of intelligence where it cannot benefit from a thoughtful and good man talking about truths and principles then he (or we) are out of this world.

To abandon preaching would be fearsome close to abandoning the spreading of the Gospel, the teaching of the beatitudes, the singing of praise to God and goodness.

Abandoning the pulpit would be yielding the rostrum to those who through the press, radio, television, public meetings and demonstrations, one way or another frequently present the very antithesis of what our churchmen want to tell us.

No, it is not a time to abandon sermons but to cut them short, bring them alive, clothe them in simple language to the melody of love and the inspiration of a good day's work.

And if our churchmen will do this, in all denominations, they may also find that they can put away talk of leaving empty churches and holing up in 'cells'."[5]

Surely the voice of God speaks to some of us through that editorial, the same voice that once said to Paul in an hour of deep discouragement, "Have no fear: go on with your preaching and do not be silenced, for I am with you ... and there are many in this city who are my people." (Acts 18:9, 10, N.E.B.)

With such encouragement from man and God we had better ask ourselves again if we believe that this is a day for the Church to stop preaching. Do we believe that the Church ought to muffle its prophetic voice and withdraw into the silence of a sterile sacramentalism and the mere activism of human betterment? Or do we believe that now as never before the Church must have something to say – not a word of opinionated preachers, but an authentic Word of God that it can proclaim with conviction, relevance and power? Even yet it may please God "by the foolishness of preaching to save them that believe".

CHAPTER NOTES

1 Elton Trueblood, *The Incendiary Fellowship* (Harper, New York, 1967), pp. 48–49.
2 Karl Borth, op. cit. p.31, *ante.*
3 Abingdon Cokesbury Press, New York and Nashville, 1949, pp. 12–13.
4 Henry Sloane Coffin, *Communion Through Preaching* (Scribner, New York, 1952), pp. 31–32.
5 In a personal letter granting permission for its use in this manuscript the editor, Mr. I. Norman Smith, said, "One does not write or publish an editorial like that without a good deal of thinking and heart searching."